**Praise for**
*The Community of Kindness*

"Kindness, like love, is eternal, and when we live it in community we weave a web of sacred connection. This lovely book is a testament to that connection, reminding us once again that it is palpable, exquisite, and unending."

—**Daphne Rose Kingma,** author of
*Coming Apart, True Love, The Future of Love*

"Bravo! What a beautiful gift to the world from the editors of Conari Press! *The Community of Kindness*, addressing our longing for connection, touched me deeply. It inspired and gave me solid ideas for inclusive, 21st-century community building."

—**Joan Steinau Lester, Ed.D.**, partner, The Equity Consulting Group and author of *Taking Charge: Every Woman's Action Guide to Personal, Political and Professional Success*

# The COMMUNITY
## of KINDNESS

# The COMMUNITY of KINDNESS

Reconnecting
to Friends, Family,
and the World
through the
Power of Kindness

The Editors of
*Random Acts of Kindness*

CONARI PRESS
Berkeley, California

Copyright © 1999 Conari Press

Conari Press books are distributed by Publishers
Group West

Cover Illustration: Kurt Vargo
Cover art direction: Ame Beanland
Cover and interior design: Suzanne Albertson

ISBN: 1-57324-148-2

**Library of Congress Cataloging-in-Publication Data**
The community of kindness : reconnecting to friends,
family, and the world through the power of kindness /
the editors of Random acts of kindness.

    p.     cm.
  ISBN 1-57324-148-2 (tradepaper)
  1. kindness.  2. Interpersonal relations.
I. Conari press  II. Random acts of kindness.
BJ1533.K5C65  1999                  98-45502
303.3—dc21                        CIP

Printed in the United States of America on recycled paper.
99  00  01  02    QUEB   10 9 8 7 6 5 4 3 2 1

Past the seeker as he prayed, came the
crippled and the begger and the beaten.
And seeing them, the holy one went down
into a deep prayer and cried, "Great God,
how is it that a loving creator can see such
things and yet do nothing about them?"
And out of the long silence, God said,
"I did do something. I made you."

—*SUFI TEACHING STORY*

# The COMMUNITY of KINDNESS

weight, and purpose of our existence, has been largely the province of academic and spiritual leaders. The rest of us have simply tried to make do, dealing as best we can with the challenges of daily life. The weightier decisions, the power and responsibility for bending the flow of history, were out of our grasp. This is no longer true, for one of the side effects of the world's growing acceptance of democracy—combined with extraordinary advancements in communications technology—has been the steady emergence of public opinion as the ultimate source of power.

Political leaders can still lead and persuade, but the days when they could bend a nation's direction to their wills are fast disappearing. World opinion has an increasingly deeper and more profound influence on the behavior of supposedly "sovereign" states. Slowly, almost outside of our range of perception, the beliefs and opinions of individuals all over the world are becoming not only more clearly articulated and understood, but more powerful.

With that increase in power comes a parallel increase in responsibility, and that too is something people are beginning to take more seriously. From the international grassroots movement to ban land mines to the extraordinary global environmental movement, individual people are assuming a greater degree of personal responsibility for worldwide issues and are acting on it to an extent unimaginable just a few decades ago. We are recognizing how interconnected we are, how much of a global community we can be, but we are uncertain what forms these connections will take.

That's because the rhythm and structure of what we know of community is centuries old. Our way of feeling connected to a place and to the people of that place has not changed significantly in the tens of thousands of years of organized human history, and now, seemingly suddenly and irrevocably, virtually every old form of community is collapsing all around us. Small towns are becoming big cities or are being swallowed up by even bigger cities; extended families are spread out across the land; ties of tribe, clan, and region have ceased to fulfill the comforting task of locating us intimately within a community. The bonds that once held us have been broken, and we are left with a disturbing unease, a sense of being cast adrift. We are no longer sure where we fit or where we can turn for comfort and a sense of belonging. In theory our community has expanded globally, but in the marrow of our bones most of us feel cut off and alone.

This is a modern human problem. For most of history, belonging to a community was taken for granted. Whether clan, tribe, small town, or big-city neighborhood, it was there people were born and raised, and it was within community that individuals struggled to find their place. The fact of community was a given; the fitting into it and the defining of the individuals within it were the issues. In our lifetimes, for the first time in history, the ground rules have shifted. We grow up with breathtakingly unlimited opportunity to find our own ways, but in increasing numbers we grow up outside the steady comfort of any true community; the absence of that all-encompassing caress leaves us feeling deeply disconnected.

*The Community of Kindness* has grown out of our experience with the "Random Acts of Kindness" movement. As the publishers of three bestselling books, we have spent a great deal of time thinking about why the *Random Acts of Kindness* series struck such a chord; why, at last count, eleven countries, 40,000 individuals, 15,000 schools, 1,000 churches, and 450 towns, cities, and counties in the United States are participating in Random Acts of Kindness week in February. As the years progressed and the kindness movement grew internationally, it became clear that the success of the books, and the desire to do good deeds, random or planned, results from the sense of community created by performing such acts. When we feed the meter of a car about to get a ticket, we connect to the person who owns that car, even if we never meet. When we leave a bouquet of flowers on a neighbor's doorstep because we've heard he's having chemotherapy, we forge a bond, if only briefly. And when we read about such actions, we connect not only to those who have performed such deeds, but to the tribe of all others who are reading about them. It is out of our longing for community that so many of us have joined the "kindness revolution."

So we at Conari decided to write a book of meditations on community itself, a book that would encourage us all to connect deeply to those who are already in our lives, to think creatively about new ways we can reach out to the wider world, and to actively participate in the creation of new forms of community that will be deeply satisfying and help make the world a better place. *The Community of Kindness* is full of stories from folks who have received or witnessed acts of kindness, as well as thoughts from a wide variety of people who are working to create community.

As we thought about and spoke to people about the notion of community, we began to see that whatever forms of community emerge over the next decades, the one absolute prerequisite for their success is simple human kindness. It is only through kindness that the fundamental human desire to

8

connect to one another will have the quality of compassion that allows us to understand and forgive the stumblings and failures of ourselves and others. It is our passionate hope that these meditations will assist us all in bringing kindness to the forefront of our lives, so that we can fulfill our longing for community in ways that better fit our changing world.

# 2

# Remembering the Kind Embrace of Community

*We are members of one great body,*
*planted by nature in a mutual love,*
*and fitted for a social life. We must*
*consider that we were born for*
*the good of the whole.*

—*Seneca*

*I*n *some deep, often unrecognized way*, each of us car-ries in our hearts a yearning for the com-munity we know has been lost—a closeness, a quality of connection to other people that sings with vibrancy and shines with vitality. This feeling calls out to us of a time and place of belonging, of comfort, of being nestled in the hands of unquestioned love and embraced by the warmth of acknowledgment and understanding; a place we can be ourselves and have impact on others; a place that feels like home.

The source of that longing is multifaceted. At its deepest level it speaks of our severance from the divine—the banishment from the garden of Eden. Once we were one, a seamless and effortless unity of love, and now there is a deep ache of emptiness. We have been thrown out and must make our own way back.

Echoing this spiritual separation is the very human separation that begins with our expul-sion from our mother's womb and continues unabated through the childhood process of individuation, until we emerge into adulthood as a separate person. It seems that, at least in

Western culture, half our life is spent separating, creating distance and boundaries so that we might know where the "I" begins and ends.

Sometimes we are given an extended experience of community during the magical time when we have left our childhood behind but have not yet emerged as adults. This is often a time of great personal openness, when we are more willing to trust, more ready to expose our hearts, more eager to assume the best of intentions and forgive the inevitable dissonance. It is often then, in our late teens and early twenties, living with friends in houses and apartments with a constant stream of people circulating through our lives, that we see for the first time what living within a true community could feel like.

Almost invariably, the unfinished work of discovering our own identity, our own needs and desires, pulls us away from these experiences of the comfort of others. For most of that journey of self-discovery, we are either too self-absorbed to notice or too easily mistake a crowd for community. All the while, however, locked away in our hearts is a deeply

# Across the Divide

*There are no great people except those who
have rendered service to humankind.*

—*Anonymous*

"When I was growing up, I was always smiling, always looking on the bright side. Even in my teens and early twenties my friends used to call me the 'cure for depression.' I can't even remember exactly how I ended up where I did—it seems like my life just unfolded badly—but by time I was thirty, I had sunk into a pretty frightening depression of my own.

"Most of my friends were avoiding me, because I was suddenly the one who needed to be cheered up. A lot of issues which had been trailing me for years, which I had been ignoring, just camped at my doorstep and wouldn't go away no matter how hard I tried to banish them. I finally realized I was supposed to actually deal with these issues, not just smile harder and pretend they'd go away. Things did improve with that realization, but it still felt like I was running in sand-every—

thing was difficult, brown, and gritty. Having given up my 'It's OK, I'm fine' routine, it now seemed I was being exiled to a world where I would never be all right again.

"Then one day heading home from work, without any conscious plan, I got off the subway a few stops early and found myself walking into a coffee shop. I remember sitting down and wondering what I was doing there, and at exactly that moment a gray-haired woman walked up to me and asked me if I was following her. I was totally flustered and sputtered out some incoherent denial. She took my hand, sat me down, ordered me a drink, and told me she had been sitting across from me in the subway and noticed that I seemed pretty distracted, and wondered if I wanted to talk about it.

"The situation took me so much by surprise that it cracked me open like an eggshell. I sat there for almost three hours talking to this woman, laughing, crying, and just feeling alive again after what seemed like a long sleep. Her reaching out to me made all the difference! While I continued to struggle for a year or so, I would remember her kindness to me and have hope."

Sometimes, it takes a total stranger to remind us how closely connected we truly are. It doesn't necessarily take a lot of work. When we can extend ourselves across the barriers that separate us, and gently touch the heart of another, it resonates like the ringing of a well-crafted bell. ❧

## Our Longing for Rootedness

*To be rooted is perhaps the most important and least recognized need of the human soul.*

—SIMONE WEIL

"I live in a very nice house just outside Chicago. When we first moved here, I was so excited. We had lived in a rented apartment downtown ever since we got married, and I had grown tired of the noise, the space limitations, having no yard, and a constant series of minor but irritating neighbor problems. One of the first things I did in our new house was to fix up the yard, which had been neglected. While I was out there digging away, some people from the neighborhood came by to welcome us and comment on the flowers I was putting in. It felt so wonderful.

"We've been here for six years now, and I still love my house and I really love working in the yard and turning it into a place of beauty, but I realized a while ago that something important was missing. At first it was hard to pin down, I just knew that somewhere in my life there was an empty place where something good was supposed to be. After flailing around (I even tried blaming my husband, but fortunately he just laughed), I finally realized that it was other people I was missing. Not anyone in particular, just friendly faces saying good morning, talking about the weather or gardening. I had everything I wanted in a neighborhood except the hum and sparkle of people just being friendly. I realized that for me, it isn't just the physical beauty and arrangement of home and garden that are important. More than anything I need to feel the sweet energy only people can provide.

"Once I decided what was missing, I set out to draw my neighbors outside their backyards a little more often. At the beginning of December, I wrote up about thirty invitations to a 'neighborhood open house' for a Sunday afternoon between three and six o'clock during the holiday season and slipped them under my neighbors' front doors. The time rolled around and my husband and I sat there, worrying if anyone would show up. Well, around forty people started swarming the place, and everyone had a great time. It was so successful that someone else volunteered to host a neighborhood swim party in the summer. And that afternoon we talked a bit about traffic problems and crime and decided to hold quarterly meetings to deal with these issues."

Sometimes all it takes is someone to get the ball rolling. If the need and desire is there, the effort doesn't have to be strenuous. If you are sitting in your house wishing to be closer to your neighbors, chances are they are feeling the same way too. Initiate a get-together and see what happens. ❧

## Creating Real Connection

*Down deep in every human soul is a
hidden longing, impulse, and ambition to do
something fine and enduring.... If you are
willing, great things are possible to you.*

—*Grenville Kleiser*

"Last year I visited Jean Claude, a French
friend I have kept in touch with over the
years. We had met in Paris when we were
both students, and he had since gone on to
become a veterinarian. About fifteen years
ago he, his wife, and their son moved to a
small village in a very rugged area of France
as a part of the 'back to the land' movement.
I remember thinking at the time that it
sounded terribly romantic and I wanted to
hurry over to get a taste of the rustic rural life.

"It took me fourteen years to get there, but
I was lucky enough to show up just in time
for the Chestnut Festival, which, in great
country style, was really just an excuse to get
the town together to eat roasted chestnuts and
drink wine under the moonlight. By the third
glass of wine, I was in full fantasy mode: This

was heaven on earth. Jean Claude just laughed. Where I was seeing the perfect, close-knit rural community, he had lived through fifteen very difficult years of trying to overcome being the outsider, seeing his farm and his marriage fail without any support from his neighbors, and finally putting some new and different pieces together again.

"'What I wanted to believe when I first moved here,' he said, 'was that this town is a good place to live—and it has become that. But when I first got here, it was very ingrown and suspicious of outsiders. At some point, everyone in town has confessed to me that they all wished that I and the rest of 'those weird university students' would just disappear. They didn't like our long hair, they didn't like our lifestyles. People didn't even begin to talk to me until my farm failed and I went back to being a veterinarian—and that was only because I was the only vet around. But slowly, as I worked with the other farmers' animals, people began to accept me and even solicit my advice.'

"At the time I was visiting, Jean Claude was

in a tight election for mayor of the town. He won, proving that he and the other 'outsiders' had done a pretty good job breaking down the old barriers. The lesson I learned on that trip have stuck with me: Real communities don't just happen because the town is small, rural, or old. Real communities have to be built, and one of the most important parts is a willingness to accept and even celebrate differences." ❧

## Going Home Again

*Our own life is the instrument with which we experiment with Truth.*

—*Thich Nhat Hanh*

"Most of my extended family had emigrated from Cincinnati to California just after World War II. My cousins and I grew up hearing our parents talk about the old neighborhood. It seemed like every time the stories were told they gained a little luster. But most of us kids thought California was the coolest place to be, and we pretty much ignored the

23

adults when they got on to their storytelling. By time we had grown, our roots were firmly West Coast, and Cincinnati was just a place our family had come from.

"So it took us by surprise when my cousin Sheila decided, a couple years after accompanying her parents on a reunion tour of Cincinnati, to move back to the old neighborhood. Her decision came at a time when her whole life was up in the air—she had just gotten laid off, her marriage, after years of limping along, had finally ended, and her kids were old enough to be out on their own. It was certainly a good time to make a change, but some of us worried that she was trying to go back to something that was no longer really there.

"Recently I stopped in to see her on the way back from a business trip to the East Coast, and the first thing out of her mouth was, 'So do I look like someone trying to bury themselves in the past?' Since that was clearly on both our minds, it proved to be the perfect icebreaker. We ended up spending a great couple of days together, me getting a tour of

Cincinnati complete with hysterically funny commentary (highlighted by her own discovery of numerous inaccuracies in our family's mythology).

"What Sheila had learned is that you can't go back in time, but that didn't change her mind about Cincinnati. In the difficult process of resettling, she made some good friends and was committed to building on that beginning. 'I didn't find what I was looking for,' she said, 'but I think I found a place where I'm comfortable trying to create something.'"

It's easy to get nostalgic for the good old days, even if they were someone else's. But we have to live in the here and now, and often nostalgia prevents us from reaching out in the moment to whoever is right in front of us, no matter where we live. ❧

# To Be of Use

*As for accomplishments, I just did what
I had to do as things came along.*

—*ELEANOR ROOSEVELT*

"In 1997, I was finishing my senior year at college and feeling out of sorts. I didn't know what I wanted to do and was getting irritated by my father, who seemed to be heading toward a major panic attack about my 'future.' I guess I was pretty self-absorbed, and I was only marginally aware that the Red River in North Dakota was overflowing its banks and threatening to flood hundreds of square miles when one of my old roommates stopped by my apartment to pick up a book he had lent me. It turned out he knew some people whose house was under water, and he had decided to head west until he hit the disaster area and then offer to help in any way he could.

"I don't know why I decided to go with him, but I did, and found myself knee-deep in floodwaters two days later. We had made it to the outskirts of Grand Fork, North Dakota, and had been scooped up into a loosely organized brigade of sandbaggers. The first day was miserable. I kept wondering how I had found myself in the middle of a freezing flood zone. I don't think my body has ever been that sore, that cold, that wet, that coated in gritty, clinging sand. By the next day, however, it had settled down into almost a routine—a numb routine—but a routine.

"It was hard, it was boring, and ultimately all our work was pretty much for nothing, as the Red River just kept pouring out over the valley, paying our little wall of sandbags no mind at all. But it seemed like the worse it got, the friendlier the people working together became There I was with a washed-out puddle of people I didn't know, and we were all laughing, talking, and hugging like we'd all know each other all our lives.

"That experience changed me. I started thinking that if dragging myself out of my self-absorption could make me feel that at that moment I belonged nowhere else but in the muddy mess of Grand Fork, then I should be able to find other ways to feel a part of something larger in my normal life. I haven't really figured out how yet, but I know it involves including other people in my life."

Often it is a crisis—a fire, an earthquake, an oil spill—that pulls us out of ourselves and encourages us to take the hand of the person next to us. And, as this young man discovered, banding together for a good cause feels good. Our challenge is to reach out when we are just zipping along the normal track of our lives. One way to do that is to keep your eyes open for opportunities that present themselves to you—whether they're across the country or around the corner. ❧

# No Contribution Too Small

*Just to be on the first step*
*should make you happy and proud.*
*To have reached this point is no small*
*achievement: what you have done*
*already is a wonderful thing.*

—C. V. CAVAFY

"For a few years, I lived in the bowels of Los Angeles working the night shift (and a double shift if I could get it) in a meat-packing factory. Needless to say, this wasn't a career choice. I needed cash and this was the fastest way I could get it. To save money I was living in a dump just a few blocks away and I'd walk to work and back. Each morning I'd pass this weird concrete planter box set in the middle of the graffiti covered concrete. Sometimes it had flowers in it and sometimes it didn't. I couldn't figure out what was going on. It became a game, trying to guess whether or not there would be flowers in the planter.

"This went on for months. Occasionally the box was empty, but always within a day or two, more flowers would appear. One day on the way home from a double shift, I saw an old woman transplanting petunias into the box.

"It must have sounded a little gruff, but the words just popped out of my mouth: 'Why do you do this?' She turned around, smiled, and said, 'Aren't they beautiful?' 'Yeah,' I said, 'and I loved the Iceland Poppies last week.' At that she smiled again and told me she had hoped they would look so fragile that no one would want to tear them out. 'So why do you do this?' I repeated. 'For you, and everyone else who has to walk down this concrete tunnel' she replied.

"I only saw her a couple more times but I saw the flowers almost every day. I can't be completely sure, but I think that after awhile, the vandalism stopped, because the planter box started to take on the look of something permanent. I will always think of that woman, for this simple act was her contribution to a better world."

It's easy to get overwhelmed into inertia by the problems in the world. But as the old woman demonstrated, all you have to do is to look around and see what small thing you can do today, within your everyday life. ❧

# Finding New Forms

*We are the ones we've been waiting for.*

—JUNE JORDAN

"I have a group of friends that gets together to talk on a regular basis, and one of the topics that always comes up is this ever-present, rarely acted-upon desire to live in a 'real community' where everybody knows everyone else and there is a deep sense of rootedness. I think we all had these softly filtered movies in our heads of walking down the street greeting everyone we meet, and going to big picnics every Sunday. A couple of years ago, Eileen, one of our group, came back from a trip to England to visit a friend.

"Her friend lived in our fantasy community, a small English town a few hours outside London. We listened with avid interest as Eileen told us about the trip. Each day seemed better than the day before. There were shopping trips in the village complete with introductions all around, invitations to tea, a dinner party, informal get-togethers. It sounded so perfect until Sunday, when

31

Eileen's friend headed off to a church she no longer believed in.

"It was the only church in town and everyone went there. Not to go would have left her squarely outside the community. And so, to avoid gossip and ostracism, she went.

"Our group recoiled in horror. Such hypocrisy, while it did seem necessary under the circumstances, seemed intolerable. We suddenly saw the downside of our fantasy—particularly the pressure to conform that insular communities can exert. Suddenly the dream seemed a bit tarnished.

"But out of our disillusionment came the realization that our group was the community we were looking for! We had been so blinded by the old form that we couldn't see what was right in front of our noses. The nine of us didn't live within walking distance, we didn't see each other every day, but we were always there for one another—adoption parties, moving days, holidays, birthdays, barbecues, house-sitting, home repairs, gardening projects. We swapped cars and video cameras, light meters and tree trimmers. We provided shoulders to cry on, places to crash, and audiences for laughter. We offered each other a variety of kindnesses on a regular basis. We were the roots that we were seeking!"

Community does provide roots, but the challenge of our times is to discover rootedness wherever we are so that we can bloom where we are planted. If you are longing for connection, how about joining a group? It can be an existing one that meets a certain need—Parents without Partners, AA, a neighborhood improvement association. Or you can just ask a few people (nine or ten is great, because even when some people can't make it, it still feels like a group) to get together to explore being in community. ❧

# We're All in This Together

*We are all part of an evolving process,*
*one that is never finished. Tribe allows us to*
*see our part in the eternal flow more clearly,*
*to be inspired by it, to be shown how*
*our lives have meaning far beyond*
*the reach of our years.*

—CAROLE KAMMEN
AND JODI GOLD

"Many years ago, my husband and I were living in North Dakota. It was a transfer situation—we had to make it through three years in the tundra before we would be eligible to transfer back to New York. That's how I thought of it at the time, but looking back, it was probably one of the most important times in my life. In our second year there, the entire state was blanketed in a series of snowstorms the likes of which my Brooklyn-born self could not even imagine. Our house was outside of town a couple of miles, which meant we were isolated from the world until the roads got plowed.

"We both managed to get home just as the

heavy snows started to fall, and were surprised when a few hours later we heard a loud knocking at our door. Standing on our front porch covered in snow were our neighbors, the Mitchells: Mom, Dad, and three kids. Unaware of the intensity of the blizzard, they had gotten turned around and ended up with their car buried in a snowbank a couple hundred yards from our house.

"For the next three days, as the snow built up into huge drifts around the house, we had the time of our lives, laughing, cooking, and talking into the early hours. We even all camped out in the living room in front of the fireplace, like a giant slumber party, to keep the youngest child from getting scared. On the fourth day the sun finally emerged onto an astonishingly beautiful winter scene. One large snow-family later, the highway department snowplows made their way down the road and towed the Mitchells' car back onto the highway.

"With hugs, waves, and promises to keep in touch, they drove off. What was funny was that when we walked back into our home, it felt empty, as if an essential part of ourselves had been lost.

"Since that day, I have gone out of my way to stay in touch with the Mitchells. We have gotten together many times, in New York and in South Dakota, and the kids, as they have grown, have each made trips to the big city to visit us. In some way, we are family."

Do you have a "tribe"? A group of people related by blood or by circumstances—old college roommates, the group that went to China together to adopt their daughters—that you are a part of? These are important sources of community, and as the story above suggests, it is often by extending kindness that a tribe gets created. ❧

# The Magic's in Us

*A good heart is better than all the
heads in the world.*

—EDWARD LYTTON

"Like a lot of people, I grew up listening to my grandmother telling stories of the 'good old days.' But unlike most people, I never got tired of the same old stories. I don't know why they affected me so strongly, whether my grandmother was a particularly good story-teller or I was just an overly romantic little girl, but her stories always held magic for me.

"It wasn't even that she always told stories about good times. But somehow imbedded in all her stories was a feeling about that time and place that made it seem special, as though all the pieces, the places, the food, the smells and sounds, and particularly the cast of char-acters, were just exactly right. They were like fairytales to me.

"My grandmother died when I was still in my teens, and as I grew older, I started to wonder whether the stories I remembered her telling were real. Many years later, I went to visit the small village in the south of Poland that my grandmother had grown up in. I'm not sure what I was expecting, maybe some echo of magic from the past, but I wanted to see it for myself and maybe ask around to see if anyone remembered my grandmother.

"The people there were very friendly and put up with my total lack of Polish, but as far as I could discover there was no one left who had known my family. Even so, I could almost feel my grandmother's presence and it was a wonderful chance to remember how special she had been for me.

"On the flight home I started thinking about some of her old stories and I realized that the magic was not about the place or even the people, it was something in my grandmother, some ability that allowed her to remain true to everything and everyone she had ever known. People live, grow old, and die, places evolve and change, but that gift, that incredible connectedness my grandmother possessed, was the magic I remember and the magic I now try to bring into my life."

We can each work such magic. One way to do it is to be present when someone is speaking to you. Today, rather than thinking about the dinner you're about to cook or sorting your mail on your desk, give one other person your full and undivided attention. You will be amazed at how they will feel—and you too. ❧

## The Anchor of Friendship

*The best thing to hold onto in
life is each other.*

—*AUDREY HEPBURN*

"This is the story of how I met my best friend. It was the first week of my freshman year at college and I was so glad to be out from under my parents' roof. My last year at home seemed like an endless stream of 'You can't do this,' 'You can't do that,' and finally I was free! I was in heaven and abusing every minute of this glorious freedom.

"Coming home from a party one night, I cut across a lawn and, in the dark, I ran smack into Heather. By the time I got back under control I noticed that she was crying and I assumed that my sore knee was the cause of her tears. I started apologizing, but it came out funny. Then she started laughing and crying and saying she wasn't crying over me since she didn't even know me.

"Feeling foolish at being laughed at by a total stranger, I demanded (nicely) to know what she was crying about. At first she wouldn't tell me but she did agree to let me walk her back to her dorm. A couple of days later I saw her at the cafeteria and she said she'd tell me why she had been crying if I promised not to laugh. I crossed my heart but had to choke back a major chortle when she told me she missed her parents. She whacked me in the arm and we've been best friends ever since.

"I think now that part of the reason we hit it off so quickly is that we were each acting out the other's 'hidden' side. She really did miss her parents, but she was also really excited about being on her own and maybe even feeling a little guilty about how excited she felt. I was way overboard on the 'woman alone in the world' act, but secretly feeling isolated and lonely. At the time it was confusing, but looking back, I see that each of us was able to support the other not only in what we knew we were feeling, but in the things we were ignoring. We both needed to find a balance in separation from, and connection to, our parents.

"Heather was my anchor. Her friendship let me drift off on my adventures—often not seeing her for days or weeks—and still find my way back to her, helping me (and her) learn about being separate and connected."

No matter what our stage of life, we all ebb and flow in the tide of separation and connection, sometimes needing to be alone, sometimes needing support from others. A great gift of friendship is the willingness to accept the separations that are necessary, by becoming the anchor to which your friend can always return. ❧

# Me and You

*Healthy boundaries are flexible enough
that we can choose what to let in
and what to keep out.*

—ANNE KATHERINE

"I have always felt lucky to be alive at this time in history. It may sound silly, but one of the major reasons I feel this way is the accessibility of psychology. I love being able to figure out why I feel the way I do. Recently I realized that I had a hard time doing anything in groups because I didn't know how to graciously set limits and state my boundaries with other people.

"In college I first lived in a dorm with five roommates—definitely fun but also pretty awkward. I ended up doing more than my share of the work and resenting everyone else. I then moved to an off-campus apartment with three roommates. That worked pretty well until one roommate got married and her replacement had a constant stream of men going in and out of the house, which I felt powerless to do anything about. After college, I decided to live alone. I loved it. In a lot of ways, living alone was absolutely necessary for me, if for no other reason than to remove all distractions. When I finally stopped reacting to the needs and demands of everyone else, I could finally figure out who I was and what I wanted. I got into therapy and learned how to state my needs and say no when I felt it.

"Now what I want more than anything else is to be surrounded by people. All kinds of people, doing all kinds of things. Old people, young people, even old roommates—well, maybe not *all* old roommates. As soon as I really became comfortable with who I was and able to say no, a door opened and I could finally say yes. Yes to life, to being with other people. I could see myself as a part of this big bumbling, stumbling mass of people, and that was not only OK, it was exciting."

To exist in community with others, we need to be able to say no as well as yes. Because if we just go along with everything, we will soon have to leave the situation in order to come back to ourselves. True kindness, to yourself and others, can be found in stating your boundaries. It tells people where you are and how far you will go. If you are comfortable with the truth of how you feel, you can state it without hostility, judgment, or attempts to change the other person. Take a little time right now to reflect on whether you can say no graciously. If not, is there someone you could learn from? ❧

## Remembering the Past, Living the Present

*For too long we ... have been looking
backward when we hear the term history.
But history is about what is emerging
and can emerge as well as what
has already emerged.*

—MATTHEW FOX

"My father told me this story. He was a relatively young man at the time and a silent audience at a reunion of his father and some old friends from 'the neighborhood.' The older men had all immigrated when they had been young

44

from small villages in Italy to Boston, and now as old men they were telling each other stories they had told many times before about the 'good old days' back in Italy. My father, who was a thoroughly Americanized member of the second generation and has some pretty good 'good old days' stories of his own, said that as he listened, the life these men had led seemed to get better and better, deeper and richer, more filled with laughter and camaraderie with each telling, until their shared past had taken on an almost mythical glow.

"Suddenly the mood was broken when my grandfather, who had remained silent during the unfolding tales, ended the session with the comment, 'Why do you tell these stories? There was very little good about those days. Don't you remember why we all left?' It was an awkward moment, but it made a deep impression on my father, and he's passed the lesson on to all his children: Don't romanticize the past. Don't let your nostalgia for the things that were good distort the rest of the picture into looking like a golden time that in fact never was."

One of our great survival traits as a species is that in our memories, bad times tend to fade, while the good times not just stick, but take on rosy hues. This is not all bad—it helps us to overcome even the worst tragedies. But it can be hazardous too. The danger in this tendency, which novelist Milan Kundera called "the unbearable lightness of being," is that we will forget the truly bad things that have happened and give over to a pure nostalgia for the past. Looking back instead of forward, we will be afraid to walk into the future.

We need to remember the past but live in the present. The next time you find yourself strolling nostalgically down memory lane, try to look at both the good and the bad. Keeping the past in perspective is an important kindness we can do for ourselves. Otherwise we can become mired in regret. ❧

# Change Is Inevitable

*Most of us are about as eager to change as
we were to be born, and go through our
changes in a similar state of shock.*

—JAMES BALDWIN

"The town I was born in is almost 150 years old, but you couldn't tell if you visited today. I'm old enough to remember what it was like before it changed, but you should hear my parents and aunts and uncles go on and on. They alternate between telling great stories of days long gone and complaining like mad about the state of things today. Last year, the town tore down what used to be the old high school, because it was falling apart and no longer needed (there is a large newer high school a few blocks down the road), and you should have heard the goings on. It was like the end of civilization as we know it.

"For the most part I ignore them all when they get onto this topic. From where I sit a lot of the changes have been pretty positive. I've got a great job at a new computer-related business that has settled in this area and I didn't have to leave to get it, and it's not polluting the river like the old factory used to. But I've learned that sometimes with relatives it's just easier to smile and keep quiet.

"One day the old refrain was getting to me, so I made some comment about at least some things being better than they were. That was instantly shouted down. But later my uncle George tracked me down. He said I shouldn't pay them much attention, it wasn't really about better or worse, it was just that they were all in mourning over a life that didn't exist any more, and they didn't know how to do it. 'This town isn't any better or worse than it's ever been,' he said, 'it's just real different.'

"As soon as he said that I began to understand how hard it was for the older generations. The town they grew up in had pretty much been the same for generations—same families, same buildings, same businesses. Then all of a sudden it was gone, swallowed up by 'progress.' The realization made me feel warmer toward my family, because I could empathize with what they were going through. I wasn't so happy about some of the changes that had been happening in my life—sending my kids to day care because we couldn't afford to have my wife stay home; the loss of the corner hamburger joint to yet another McDonalds. . . . Sometimes I just want to turn the clock back myself."

It seems things are changing faster and faster these days, so fast that we can forget how difficult change can be, how easy it is to get polarized, and how important it is to hold on to the treasures from our past as we move into the future. ❧

# Beyond Sameness

## Celebrate Diversity!

——*BUMPER STICKER*

"I was reading an article the other day about the death of small towns all across the Midwest—complete with pictures of boarded-up shops and, old people rattling around in a town once filled with families. The article focused on towns that had sprung up across America's farmland a day's ride distance from one another and with freeways roaring by, no longer had any reason to exist other than to house the people who lived there.

"You could not read the article without feeling the loss. Small-town America is disappearing. Even in places not losing all their populations to the cities, the small towns are becoming suburbs and small metropolitan areas in their own right. And with the change has come all the problems we're so unhappily familiar with—crime, noise, pollution, people not knowing their next-door neighbors, political haggling over taxes and civic improvements. No wonder it feels like things are 'going to hell in a handbasket.'

"But then I think about my Aunt Ethel, who grew up in one of those small towns and was frozen out when she had the 'bad graces' to bring home from college an African American husband. Ethel was a gracious woman who knew what she'd lost, the closeness and the shared history but, remarkably, she never held a grudge. 'They weren't mean people,' she would say. 'They just hadn't grown to the point where they could see the different colors in God's family.'

"Our old communities, the small towns and old neighborhoods that until just a few decades ago made up the heart of American society, were for the most part built around sameness—we were all farmers, or all Italians, or all poor whites. We lived surrounded by our own kind. It was a comfort at times, but, like my Aunt Ethel said, it was OK then because that was before we had to grow up."

We are in a difficult transition period, trying to share our sameness and celebrate our differences at the same time. Too far in one direction and we whitewash over all the cultural, social, ethnic, racial, and class differences that make us unique. Too far in the other direction and we fractionalize into groups that end up believing that the "other" is less than human. We must engage our hearts and minds to somehow find the middle way, the way between either/or. Kindness and compassion are our guides through this very tricky terrain. ❧

# 3

# The Path to Community

Hope is a state of mind, not of the
world. Hope, in this deep and powerful
sense, is not the same as joy that things
are going well, or willingness to invest in
enterprises that are obviously heading for
success, but rather an ability to work for
something because it is good.

—VÁCLAV HAVEL

*I*t is difficult to describe this thing that we long for. It is an amorphous, ever-shifting need to bond with others rather than an identified destination. We use words like *community* and *connection*, but it is bigger. It is a state of being, a way of living in relationship to the whole.

The history of our species has been the story of our struggle to live together, a continuous cycle of evolving definitions of "we" and "they." For the earliest small family groups and tribes, everyone else was "other," to be feared, excluded, protected against, or conquered. Gradually tribes expanded and created larger extended alliances, which grew to loose confederations of "a people" occupying a definable region. There in turn grew to city-states, small kingdoms, larger realms, and finally nation states. Today much of the world continues to carve itself into smaller and smaller parts, reinforcing the notion of "us" against "them." At the same time, however, much of Western Europe is abolishing those things that divide, like boundaries, tariffs, and currency. We have even begun to speak seriously of the world as a "global village."

When we look out on our world we see what looks like the collapse of community, but this simply reflects our place in a larger cycle of change. Something always must die in order for something new to be born. In nature we not only accept this, we marvel at its beauty as the seasons unfold in their time-less rhythm: the fresh birth of spring, the vibrant growth and blossoming of summer, the gradual withering death of autumn, and the cold silent sleep of winter. But in society, in the institutions that frame, structure, and give meaning to our lives, the cycle of change is often difficult to keep in perspective and painful to live through.

We can see beauty in the birth and blos-soming of exciting new institutions and forms of community, but we do not view the breakdown and collapse of the comfortable furnishings of our culture with the same awe with which we view the first winter's storm. The change frightens us in the same way the onslaught of winter frightened our primitive ancestors.

Our job is to have hope and to sift through

the past to learn about what works and what doesn't, what worked and what didn't (and why), so that we can lend both our vision and our shoulder to the task of building new and better forms of community.

# Overcoming Ignorance

*You see things; and you say, 'Why?'*
*But I dream things that never were;*
*and I say 'Why not?'*
—GEORGE BERNARD SHAW

"Thirty years ago I was a guest of honor at the 'Olympic Day' festivities in a tiny village in the mountains of Japan. It was somewhat of an accident that I was there at all, but when I showed up at the local temple with a letter of introduction from a friend in Tokyo, the priest decided it was too good an opportunity to pass up. The festival is a very popular annual event in Japan, when communities or companies hold Olympic-style games. Up in the mountains the festival had a real rural charm, with events for kids under eight as well as a senior division (including a senior citizen three-legged race that was a crack-up). I was entered into a tag-team relay event where you'd run to a water barrel, fill up a big sake bottle, deliver it back to your next teammate, who would then run back to the barrel and empty the bottle, and then you would repeat that until you were soaked to the bone or the judge said the race was over.

"I was the first American ever to visit this village, and the real reason I was invited was that the priest hoped that my public and enthusiastic participation in the festival would have some healing effect on an old man who belonged to the temple. The old man had been a soldier in World War II and had emerged with some serious psychological problems. The day after the festival the priest and I paid a short visit to the old man— I smiled and nodded and he nodded a little but mostly avoided looking at me. We stopped at the elementary school on the way back to the temple and I was mobbed by laughing little kids who were more than anxious to make me their new best friend.

"I never did find out if my presence helped the old man, but the whole experience had a powerful effect on me. My father spent most of World War II in the Pacific, fighting the Japanese, and here I was, not only genuinely and warmly welcomed into this small Japanese community, but asked to participate in the healing process of one of their members. Somehow just the thought that so much hatred and fear could change so quickly into laughter and acceptance made me realize what an extraordinary capacity we have for overcoming our own ignorance."

It's so easy to make a person or a group of people our enemy. It doesn't require a war—we know sisters who refuse to speak, coworkers who are at one another's throats, neighbors who participate in escalating feuds. Is there someone in your life you've made "the enemy"? Is it possible for you to reach out and make a gesture of connection—a phone call, a postcard, a bouquet on the doorstep? ❧

# Take Matters into Your Own Hands

*See everything. Overlook a great deal.*
*Improve a little.*
—*POPE JOHN XXIII*

In sprawling metropolitan areas, there is a constant flow of traffic through residential neighborhoods as commuters desperately seek a magical shortcut that will get them out of the traffic jams and to work or back home more quickly. What is often overlooked is the frightening toll this can take on an otherwise quiet and peaceful neighborhood. One group of people came up with an innovative approach that gives us a glimpse of people can do when they come together for a common purpose.

The street in question is a narrow road through forested foothills. It's a wonderful place to live, but unfortunately it is also a convenient shortcut from the main commuting arteries. Morning and late afternoon, the otherwise quiet street is split asunder by a fast-moving swell of speeding cars. After years of trying to get the local government and transportation officials to come up with a solution, the neighbors took matters into their own hands—or more precisely, their children's hands. The people in each home along the route had their kids create large posters with a personal plea for drivers to slow down. The posters were all colorful, hand-lettered, and personal, and were posted in front yards so that drivers could read them as they sped by.

The result was immediate and dramatic. Most speeding commuters never stopped to think they might be negatively effecting the people who lived on the street, but the unfolding stream of personal pleas from the neighborhood kids was unavoidable and unignorable. Traffic slowed to a reasonable pace and even diminished over time as the drivers realigned their own priorities.

We all need to think creatively about what we can personally do, and how we can connect with others to bring about change. Often the best results emerge when people get together to see what they can do there and then. ❧

# Getting Along

*Give the world the best you have and the
best will come back to you.*

—*MADELINE BRIDGES*

"I remember the excitement I felt at the
end of my freshman year in college when
three close friends and I signed a lease on the
house we would share next school year. My
freshman roommate experience had been the
pits, but I blamed the school for that—my
assigned roommate and I had absolutely
nothing in common. But next year was going
to be fabulous: our own house, three bedrooms, our own kitchen, a front porch, a living room big enough for a decent-sized
gathering.

"In fact, it was a pretty good year, but I sure
learned a lot about dealing with other people.
One of my roommates was completely irre-
sponsible about money, as in 'our' money. In
only our second month as rent-payers, he had
already squandered his check from home and
we had to front his share. Then we'd buy food,
he'd eat it, and never get around to replacing it.

"There was constant fighting over who had to share a bedroom. That got really complicated with issues like who had 'found' the house in the first place, who had a regular girlfriend (that one cut both ways, particularly if she had a decent housing situation), and who did the most work around the house. There were the endless arguments about meals (free for all versus sharing some meals); tasks (clean house versus who cares anyway); music, which we usually all agreed on but fought over when and how loud to play; and the host of little but irritating habits that anyone brings to any situation. Up until then the only people I had ever lived with were family, and I never realized how hard it could be to fit yourself into a rhythm with other people."

Whether living with others, working day-to-day in the office, or coming together for a neighborhood project, we can easily get bogged down in all the ways that other people annoy or frustrate us. It seems easier to just sit home alone in front of the TV or computer screen. But if we want to break out of our isolation, we need to go beyond our annoyance. To do so, we need to respect our differences (some people are quiet and others loud; some messy and others neat; some quick and others slow) and negotiate through the rough spots. Neither talent is well developed in our society.

This is where kindness comes in. The more we are kind to one another, the more we can negotiate problems in good faith, and the more smoothly our "community" (home, office, club) will run. ❧

# True Respect

*When we shun or judge people because of*
*their differences, we cut ourselves off from*
*a few of life's pleasant surprises.*
—*BOBBIE M.*

"I work in an office with twenty people who put out a weekly newspaper that, among other things, encourages kindness and community, and boy, do we struggle to practice what we preach. All of the people are good-hearted and believe in treating one another well. But somehow, over and over, no matter who is hired, the staff has a tendency to fractionalize, with backbiting, gossip, and snide looks.

"I've thought about where this behavior comes from, and I've concluded that the root of the problem is a lack of true respect for our differences. It's one thing to pay lip service to the idea that we are all different; it is another to bump up actively against those differences day after day in a tolerant and accepting manner.

"People tend to divide up according to their differences and can't see that everyone's contribution is important. Those who are quiet, methodical, rational 'loners' are constantly frustrated and put off by the more flamboyant, chaotic, intuitive workers, while the loud and off-the-cuff types have trouble seeing that the quiet workers are doing anything at all. Both groups are convinced that the office would be perfect if we just fired the other group and hired people just like them. But to put out a good newspaper we need both—the methodical folks who see to all the details, and the creative, innovative workers to give the content spark and relevancy. Without both, we would have a paper that quickly lost energy or went broke because the bills were never collected."

The ability to see what's good about another human being's annoying or frustrating behavior is a great skill for getting along in community, whether that is a work situation, a love relationship, dealing with your children, anywhere. For the truth is that there is always something good about *every* behavior. Frustrated about your son's laziness? Bet he is great at relaxing, a skill that's very important in today's busy world. Annoyed at her fastidiousness? We bet a penny never gets lost in her budget.

Today, take a few minutes to open your heart and look for the good in the behavior of someone who really bugs you. How is the very thing that drives you crazy helpful to you? To the community the two of you are a part of? ❧

# Insiders and Outsiders

*The law imprinted on the hearts of all people is to love the members of society as themselves.*

—ROMAN GOLDEN RULE

"It always makes me a little nervous when people talk about community, because I remember so strongly feeling outside of the community I grew up in. I never went to college. We didn't have the money, and my father was very sick, so I stayed at home to work and help my mom take care of Dad. This was back in the late sixties and early seventies when it seemed like everyone else in my age group was growing their hair long, protesting, and having more fun than I was.

"I may have been cut off from what my contemporaries were doing, but that didn't mean I felt any different. I just didn't have the comforting presence of a lot of people around me who shared my beliefs. Most of my world was made up of people my parent's age—the 'silent majority,' as it was referred to back then. So there I was a closet antiwar kid (much too timid to actually say anything) at dinner parties with people who wanted to bomb Vietnam out of existence and thought Richard Nixon was the be-all and end-all of presidents.

"I didn't fit in and I knew it, but they all treated me as a 'good young person,' which somehow validated their opinions about everything. I felt like a traitor. What I never felt was comfortable. It finally came crashing down the day the Ohio National Guard fired real bullets into the protesting students at Kent State. One of my father's friends was visiting at the time and made some comment about those 'damned students.' Something inside me cracked. I ran to my room and cried for hours. I'm ashamed to say it wasn't out of grief for those poor students; it was just pure sadness, loneliness, and fear. My world was very lonely, and the community I lived in was scary, not a comfort at all."

In any community, there is always the potential for exclusion and prejudice. A community built on intolerance may feed our preconceptions and bring us some comfort, but it offers us little real connection. Being a minority at the mercy of an insensitive community can be a frightening experience.

For a moment, think about the communities you are a part of—work, church, neighborhood, club. Do they welcome a diversity of people and opinions? Or are they exclusive and intolerant of disagreement? If the latter is true, is there something you can do to bring a more welcoming atmosphere? Is there someone on the outside of your community who would delight in your reaching out? ❧

# The Shadow Side

*To work in the world lovingly means that we are defining what we will be for, rather than reacting to what we are against.*

—CHRISTINA BALDWIN

It's easy to get carried away when talking about community. It's one of those magic words that is always used in a positive sense. We talk about building a strong community, serving the community, getting the support or approval of the community. Even the word itself has a warm, secure, and encompassing feel to it. But we must remember that a community that is bound together for the wrong reasons can be a very dangerous thing.

We have many examples to learn from, such as cults like the People's Temple and Heaven's Gate that misused the strong bonds of community to force people's lives and beliefs into tightly controlled pathways, and sectarian political parties either far left or far right, who dictate behavior, lifestyle, and goals for members. Certainly one of the most dramatic and frightening examples of the misuse of community bonds was the power-ful nationwide community-building under-taken in Nazi Germany.

The extent to which the Nazis were suc-cessful in building a strong sense of commu-nity among the German people was rare in world history, and that very success made Nazi Germany a powerful and feared force in the world. The politics of hatred are meaning-less and impotent until they are united with the force of a real and viable community.

We need to be ever mindful of the danger of a community based on overly narrow or immoral principals. Community makes it possible to marshal and focus a vastly greater flow of human energy than one individual can—it makes it possible to accomplish things no individual could imagine. Yet, that very potential can be, and has been, used just as easily for evil as for good. Community is not a self-contained goal; it is merely a form of human connection. The moral basis and underlying purpose of the community are what are truly important.

In every group we join or create, whether

it be family or corporation, church or civic organization, we need to ask ourselves: What is our guiding vision? What is our mission? How well do we deal with differences? Are we an open group; that is, do people flow in and out? Is there space for new perspectives and uncomfortable questions? ❧

## Making Our Dreams Come True

*From where you are, from who you are*
*in your everyday life, that's where*
*you make change.*
—*TOSHI REAGON*

"My mother is part of a group of older women who live year-round on Cape Cod and call themselves 'The Beach Club,' although, they claim, they've never been to the beach. Once a month they get together at someone's house for lunch and talk. Sometimes they go to a museum or the theater. When a spouse dies or someone is sick, they are right there for one another, casserole and flowers in hand. My mother formed the club by asking all the women she knew and liked from various other contexts—church, garden club, the YMCA—to meet one day at her house. It turned out that they all had a lot in common, and so the group stuck."

One of the fascinating things about the time we are living in is that around the world, people are finding new ways of coming together, and reviving old ones to fit the times. Whether in twelve-step programs, spirituality circles described in books such as *Wisdom Circles* and *Sacred Circle,* "Living Tribes" as discussed in the book *Call to Connection,* reading groups, Internet chat rooms, or informal groups like "The Beach Club," people are creating intentional communities of all sorts, shapes, and sizes.

But because such coming together is not "news," we don't hear about this phenomenon, and we can easily fall into despair, believing all the bad news about the decay of our communities that we hear on TV every day. To avoid such despair, we can pay attention to the things that are breaking through in the world instead of just those that are breaking down. Several newspapers and magazines, such as *Good News* and *Hope*, report on the positive things that are happening in the world, as does the book *Stone Soup for the World*. Futurist Barbara Marx Hubbard believes it is so important to find out what's working that she has created a Web site to publicize such good news: www.cocreation.org.

Look around at your own life and those of your coworkers, friends, and family. What groups do you belong to? How well are they functioning? ❧

## Passing It On

*Live and learn—and pass it on.*

—ANONYMOUS

"A few years ago I got transferred out of the laid-back accounting department I had worked in for four years and into the financial department at corporate headquarters. It was meant as a vote of confidence in my abilities but I was not at all sure I wanted to go. I had heard lots of rumors about my soon-to-be boss Fred, how he was a stickler for detail and a complete perfectionist. Sure enough, the very first day I got called into his office and he explained to me that in his department there was no room for error. I was ready to pack my things, but I stayed, and over the next two years I got the best education I could ever have imagined.

"Fred took it upon himself to turn me into someone who could plan and execute a wide spectrum of reports with a very high degree of confidence in the numbers. Frankly he had more faith in my ability that I did. But even more, he taught me how to manage people and how to work cooperatively with colleagues in a complex corporate environment. In the process, he taught me an awful lot about myself.

"After two years, I received a job offer from another company, and the offer was something I really could not refuse. But I felt like a traitor and I was afraid to tell Fred. When I finally got up the nerve, it turned out he had given my name to a friend of his as someone worth pursuing—he had even gotten me this new job! I couldn't believe it and when I told him how much I appreciated all he had done for me, he said my only responsibility was to pass it on.

"When Fred was very young, he had dropped out of school to get a job because both his parents were unemployed. He was taken under the wing of a man named Henry, who owned the store Fred worked in. Henry had never gone to school, but he was convinced that it was the way to go, and he taught Fred, badgered him, and supported him throughout a long journey of night schools and job searches. After Henry died, Fred felt the best way to repay him would be to create a legacy to Henry's kindness by mentoring as many people as he could. It is an honor to see myself as a part of that widening circle of Henry's legacy, and in my new job, I have looked for ways to pass it on myself."

No matter who we are, as we grew up and learned how to get along in the world, we had help along the way, from teachers, loving friends, maybe even a tough boss. A wonderful way to repay the kindness of such role models is to be a mentor to a young person. In this way, we participate in a great cycle of community—learning as youth, teaching as elders.

Is there someone you can help by taking them under your wing? If so, do it. If not, make a commitment to do it, and the right person soon will magically come along. ∿

## It's Already Happening

*Therefore, find your own way,
open your treasure house, invent your
own answer to the chaos.*

—GERTRUDE STEIN

"I recently adopted a baby from China and am finding out that there are concentric circles of communities. The smallest, inner circle is the group of eight families who made the two-week journey with me in January. In some real way, our daughters are sisters to one another—born around the same time in the same geographic area and going to the same orphanage. Then there is the circle of people in the community where I live, who meet once a month for two hours, and, moving outward, the larger circles of people in the region, the country, the world, who are linked together via e-mail, newsletters, and the awareness that although each of our daughters' stories and trajectories is different, we all share certain sorrows and joys, fears and dilemmas, customs and rituals. Then there is the largest circle, which connects us all, parents, daughters, and extended families, back to China itself.

"Each of us can enter any of these circles, to find conversation about attachment problems, vaccinations, cultural and language issues, developmental delays-you name it. It gives me a wonderful sense of community, even if I never meet most of the people who help me, and my daughter, along the way."

Looking around, it's easy to believe that community is dying and not being reborn. The old form of community, based solely on one's neighborhood, is in many places indeed passing away. In its place, instead of through connections based on geography, people are coming together across distances over common issues: a love of fly fishing or whiskey, the difficulties in parenting without a partner or dealing with an addicted spouse. Specialty magazines, such as *Popular Mechanics* or *Tennis*, speak to these long-distance communities that share common interests, and the Internet has greatly accelerated the trend. Now, regardless of space or time, we can join a virtual community of people who are interested in the same things we are.

Virtual or actual, our communities just don't look the way they used to. But that doesn't mean they're not alive and well. Take a moment to reflect on the kinds of communities you belong to now. What are their forms? ❧

# Finding a Balance

*It is not who is right, but what is right,*
*that is of importance.*

—*Thomas Huxley*

"Back in the early seventies I joined up with a number of friends who were interested in organic farming. We pooled our resources, rented a large farm, and enthusiastically dove in. It was hard work and we made a lot of mistakes, but it was exciting and very rewarding—especially when we got our first crop of vegetables into local stores.

"The first year there were eleven of us and while it was pretty chaotic, it was also almost always enjoyable. By our third year, we were able to support ourselves from our produce, had developed a presence in the local market, had grown to twenty-six people, and had started fighting over all kinds of issues. Should we continue to grow? Should we open our own store in town? Should we ban processed food from our kitchen? Should we require community members to be vegetarians? Nonsmokers? You get the idea. I left at the end of that year when things broke down into a struggle between two competing factions, both of whom I though were being ridiculously dogmatic.

"One of the worst aspects of that whole experience for me was that for years afterword I not only wouldn't live with anyone else, I didn't want to belong to anything that meant I'd have to get along with others. My first brush with a real community almost turned me into a hermit."

A community can be built from its beginning upon ill-founded principals; an idealistic community can become overly controlling and punitive. In any community this is a difficult and delicate balance. By definition, a community must have some shared purpose and by extension, some agreed-upon rules. Yet, historically, the temptation for any community to impose its collective will upon its individual members is strong. That is why so many of us who experimented with communal living and businesses in the seventies have backed away from groups ever since.

Most of us will not live on a farm with

twenty other people, but issues of balancing the needs and wishes of the individual versus those of the group are the same whether you are trying to build a park in your neighborhood or starting up a computer company. To work well together, we need to keep our eye on the desired outcome—and treat one another as respectfully as possible. ❧

## Peering into the Future

*The grand essentials to happiness in this life*
*are something to do, something to love,*
*and something to hope for.*

—JOSEPH ADDISON

"I was driving though San Francisco one Saturday when I saw some kind of festival going on in a park. I stopped and wandered over for a closer look. I ended up staying for two hours. The centerpiece of the event was a performance by the San Francisco Mime Troupe, but that appeared to be only the excuse for the gathering. Handfuls of musicians clustered in different parts of the park with people dancing and singing, another group of people had erected a Maypole and were weaving all comers into the dance. Picnics were scattered all around, a large clump of moms and dads huddled around a mass of children crowding the swings and slides.

"In great Bay Area style, the crowd was about as eclectic and international as you could imagine, with people of all different colors and lifestyles represented (including a tourist from Ohio I sat with for a while). I had a great time, and as I was driving home, I started thinking about all the changes that have taken place in just the last fifty years since I was born. I do that a lot, but usually I end up getting more and more depressed. This time I got excited. A gathering like that just wouldn't have been possible fifty years ago, and now it is a regular occurrence.

"I want to believe that what I experienced in that park is just a precursor to the kind of world that is emerging. Where difference is not feared, but celebrated. Where a person's color, size, shape, language, or lifestyle is seen as stimulating and interesting, not intimidating or threatening. I felt excited to be alive now, at the time when such richness of diversity is possible."

We all need visions of the future to give us hope. In your life, when you look around you, what gives you hope? ❧

## Learning to Love

*The world is not a playground;*
*it's a schoolroom. Life is not a holiday but*
*an education. And the one eternal question for*
*us all is how better we can love.*

—HENRY DRUMMOND

"I lived in Chicago for a few years during my late twenties and early thirties. It was a pretty good time but roommate issues were a constant hassle. I found a really great place, but I couldn't afford it by myself. I knew I wouldn't have trouble finding a roommate since the apartment was a major draw, but the process was so much more difficult than I thought it would be. Interviewing total strangers was just weird. I realized quickly that I didn't have a clue how to figure out who would work out.

"I finally settled for a guy who seemed decent and responsible—he lasted three weeks and moved to Costa Rica. Then I had a string of bad luck with four different roommates in a year. I was beginning to wonder if I'd ever find anyone I could live with when Stan showed up.

"I almost blew it, because my recent string of disasters had made me pretty gun-shy, and at our first meeting I got a little carried away with questions and the house rules, because later he told me I seemed like such an uptight jerk he almost walked at that point. Instead he moved in and we very quickly became close friends.

"It's not like everything was perfect, but because we really liked each other, we found ways to work things out. He put up with my depressed girlfriend and I learned Stan's rules of kosher, which were a pain but then again not really such a big deal.

"I had never really thought about all the

things that went into fitting more than one life in the same space. In a way, the couple of years we spent together made it easier for me when I started living with the woman who became my wife."

From birth, we learn the skills of community: sharing, tolerance, consideration for others, doing our fair share, anticipating what needs to be done without being told. In short, we learn the skills of love. Some of us may arrive in adulthood more schooled than others, but the lessons never end. Today, take a moment to think about the greatest lessons you've had about getting along in community. What were they and who taught them to you? ❧

# New Families

*Love that is hoarded molds at last*
*Until we know some day*
*The only thing we ever have*
*Is what we give away.*

—LOUIS GINSBERG

"When I was growing up, we lived two blocks away from my grandparents' house (reachable in under four minutes by running children). It was like Grand Central Station; there were always people there, and you were almost assured of seeing your entire extended family at least once a week. Between the never-ending supply of food and hugs, the huge backyard, and just the excitement of all the comings and goings, it was the place to be.

"I remember that time so clearly, it seemed like it had always been that way and always would. Of course that wasn't true. By the time we kids were in high school, the visits grew less frequent. After my grandfather died, my grandmother moved into a condominium across town.

"Now we kids are scattered across the

country and have families of our own. We still get together for Thanksgiving and special occasions, but the days when we were one large family are long gone. Sometimes I really miss that closeness, but it is hard to think what choices I would have made differently. I love my job and my house, even if there aren't small armies of nieces and nephews running through. I guess, in a way, my idea of family has changed. The truth is I don't think I'd like it if my brothers, sisters, parents, or cousins were as much a part of my life as they were back then. At the same time, it feels like I've lost something and I'm not sure how to find it again."

As families have gotten more mobile, most of us live far away from our "blood" relations. For many of us, this is not a bad thing; abuse or neglect in childhood has made us purposefully distance ourselves from relatives. For others, the distance is an unhappy consequence of career decisions. So, if not with our family, where do we find that closeness we crave? For some it is with a spiritual circle; for others it is with a set of close friends; for still others it is an Internet discussion group. One single mom we know has created a family with four neighbors who have kids about the same age. They share baby-sitting and meals once a week.

The forms are changing, but the feelings are the same. It's still all about love. ❧

## Reaching across the Divide

*He who wants to do good knocks at the gate;*
*he who loves finds the gate open.*

—*RABINDRANATH TAGORE*

"I always enjoyed my father's story about his sister's wedding. My father's family lived in the Spanish section of St. Louis, which at that time was a very tight community. His sister had broken all sorts of unspoken rules by dating a guy from the German neighborhood, and then really set tongues to wagging by agreeing to marry him. According to the story, it was one of the largest weddings ever held in St. Louis, because every Spaniard showed up to see if she would really marry a

German, and every German showed up to see if he would really marry a Spaniard.

"The first time I heard the story, I realized that it never occurred to me that my uncle Charles was different from my other relatives, and it certainly never occurred to me that anyone would really care what you were. Here we were, only one generation down the road, and both our sense of self-identity and our sense of who was 'foreign' had changed dramatically.

"Thinking about it now I realize that many of the prejudices that were terribly real and powerful during my father's youth aren't even an issue for my generation. I think that is an important thing. It makes building a sense of community more complicated, but it creates the potential for the results to be so much richer."

Recently we read a scientific article which explained that there is no biological basis for the belief that human beings are of different races. The visual differences among us—skin and hair color, hair texture, nose and lip shapes—are biologically like the difference between a red tulip and a yellow tulip. Race, they say in the article, is an idea of ours, and the differences we attribute to race are mostly cultural, regional, and social. To prove it, they note that the concept keeps changing. Until the mid-twentieth century, for example, Italians and Irish were considered different races; now they are considered "white." We want to believe the differences are vast, the article says, and convincing folks that race is all in our heads is like Galileo trying to convince people the Earth revolves around the sun.

What does it mean to you, personally, to think of race as an idea we humans have just made up? ❧

# Finding Our Aliveness

*Don't worry about what the world wants*
*from you, worry about what makes you come*
*more alive. Because what the world really*
*needs are people who are more alive.*

—*Lawrence Le Shan*

"When I was a child my family used to relocate to this beautiful lake for the summer. It was like moving into a different world. Most of the cabins around the lake had been owned by the same families for years, so the first week of summer each year was a big reunion as everyone arrived and unpacked. From there we moved into the rhythm of the summer: regular swimming hours, long hikes and made-up adventures, picnics and weekly barbecues (always on the weekend for the convenience of those dads who were commuting). By the end of the summer, families began filtering back to the city and the sad process of saying good-bye would roll around.

"When I think back on those times now, I realize that what we had was a community that used to reconstitute itself each year. People would come and people would leave, but each summer a new community would spring into existence and then disappear altogether. My family no longer owns the cabin, so I don't even know if this regularly re-emerging summer community is as vibrant as I remember it, but a few years ago I went back to the lake in winter. The hills were all covered in snow, all the cabins were sealed up and silent, and the only sound was the sound of wind through the trees. It was incredibly beautiful and incredibly sad."

The experience of being a part of a community can be so powerful that its absence feels like a deep wound. That's useful, because the pain reminds us that it's important to be connected to others. But at the same time, we can get stuck looking backward, mourning what is lost or even trying to reconstruct something that cannot be put back together again.

For the woman in this story, the summers at the lake were about another time. Our challenge is to find the places in our lives today where we are open to the company of others. Maybe we can't stop working for the entire summer, but we can work to build a community swimming center with picnic grounds in our neighborhood. Or make an early morning ritual of joining the same three folks at the gym for a workout and coffee.

The deep stream of aliveness is always there, waiting for us to come together and dip into it. ❧

# 4

# The Power of Kindness

There are great souls who practice
every sort of mortification from
childhood, but I am not like them.
All I did was to break my self-will,
check a hasty reply, and do little
kindnesses without making a
fuss about them.

—*SAINT THÉRÈSE OF LISIEUX*

As we assess the lessons learned from the past and imagine the community of the future, we must first return to the very foundation of all human interaction—kindness. For kindness, the deep compassion of our heart, is a fundamental requirement for any community.

Kindness can be easy to overlook. When we encounter it we often take it for granted, as if we somehow know that it will always be there and we can pay it little heed. Yet it is our overlooking of this great gift that fuels the forces of disintegration, alienation, and disconnection.

The energy of all that we as a species have brought into the world rests in our use or disuse of kindness and compassion. Kindness is the secret password whereby we recognize our connection to one another. Kindness is the vehicle for all positive human interaction, and the absence of kindness, the opportunity for all our crimes. You cannot touch it or see it, but it is the essence of human energy. Like electricity, it pulses through its pathways, vibrant with potential.

When we smile and say good morning to a stranger on the street, for example, we activate the energy of kindness and experience a momentary connection of hearts. In that moment, we acknowledge that we are here together sharing this place and time, and we feel the comforting energetic tingle of things being right in the world. If instead we turn away without offering our greeting, the energy fades, we contract and become smaller, colder, and more isolated. When we make small talk with the bagger at the supermarket, hold the door for a burdened shopper, give someone the time of day, let another car merge into our lane, listen to the complaints of a coworker—every time we move outside of our self-involvement and connect with another person, no matter how briefly, the pulsing thread of human energy ties us together. Without it we drift further and further apart.

Because kindness is so integral to our lives, it is often difficult to see its importance. But try to imagine a day without it. The result would be a barren unfolding of events with only the most sterile interactions—complete isolation. Conversely, the more kindness we bring into our lives, the more we feel fully integrated, alive, and connected to others. From this sense of overflow, we naturally want to reach out even more and do the difficult work of staying connected even when it might feel easier to let go.

# The Warmth of Belonging

*Kindness, sweetest of the small notes*
*in the world's ache, most modest and gentle*
*of the elements, entered man before history*
*and became his daily connection.*
*Let no man tell you otherwise.*

—CARL RAKOSI

"Some years ago I went to visit an old friend who was living in Paris. The first day of my visit, he walked me around his neighborhood, showing me the best bakery, produce shop, café, and restaurants, stopping to introduce me to people we'd meet along the way. Unfortunately he was unable to get off work after that, so he'd leave early in the morning and I'd get up for a leisurely morning routine and then set off exploring the wonders of Paris.

"Without really noticing it, I found myself leaving the neighborhood around his apartment later and later each day, and returning from my adventures earlier and earlier. It wasn't that I didn't find all the attractions of Paris stimulating, it was just that I felt really comfortable in his neighborhood. I'd walk down to the bakery in the morning to pick out a breakfast pastry and be greeted by smiles and salutations from shopkeepers and people on the streets; word had gotten out that I was visiting John, and I was already a member, if only temporarily, of the neighborhood. I'd linger at the café talking to people, have lunch at one of the local restaurants, and eventually head out for a day's sightseeing. When I left two weeks later, it felt like I had lived there for years and was leaving old friends."

A big city can be a very lonely place, especially for an outsider. You can walk around and observe but you are always on the outside—unless, of course, you are invited in. The simplest gestures, a smile or greeting on the street, a hearty "Good morning," a curiosity and willingness to include, can turn loneliness and exclusion into an extraordinary experience of warmth and inclusion.

No matter where you are, you can offer a smile, word, or nod of connection and warmth to whoever crosses your path. You never know what they might be going through and what that acknowledgment might mean to them. And chances are you will feel even more a part of wherever you are, home or away. ❧

## Ready to Act

*When we quit thinking primarily about ourselves and our self-preservation, we undergo a truly heroic transformation of consciousness.*

—JOSEPH CAMPBELL

"Californians are used to the ground shaking, but for the most part tornadoes are something we see on the news, not out the back window. So it was quite a shock this year when the town I live in was hit by a couple of mid-sized tornadoes. Almost immediately people started to filter into the shocked neighborhood to help sort through the piles of debris. Fortunately no one was killed or injured, but several houses were severely damaged. Local stores donated supplies to the people affected, and help in the form of money and labor started flowing in from all around the area. My house was fine, for which I give thanks, but the best feeling of all was seeing how kind everyone was. It made me feel so wonderful to know that people care."

Outpourings like this are repeated all over the world virtually every time a disaster strikes. It seems as though people are just waiting for an opportunity to help others. On the one hand, it is a powerful reminder of our capacity for compassion and generosity, but at the same time, it forces us to wonder why it takes a tragedy to bring out the best in people.

There is no simple answer. Certainly news reports of natural disasters can distort reality. Not because they report the outpouring of generosity, but because news reports make it seem as though people are kind only during disasters, when in fact many folks help others every the day of the year. The occurrence of a tragedy automatically makes news, and the assistance that's offered to the victims of the tornado, fire, or flood is also captured in the bright lights.

The sheer force of a public disaster reminds us just how fragile our existence is and just how deeply we depend on one other's support. We get shaken out of our preoccupation with our own concerns and are able to see more clearly the strong ties of community that bind us together. During these times we act like heroes. We act on behalf of others and in doing so, we see in vivid color that the single most important requirement for any sense of community is kindness. ❧

# Doing Good Is Good for You

*We will no longer be focused on only the
reduction of symptoms or the removal of
something negative, and instead begin to
understand health and well-being as the
presence of something positive.*

—*Brendan O'Regan,*
*on the future of medicine*

A fascinating topic of research is the current inquiry into the relationship between what scientists call "social helpfulness" and good emotional and physical health. Scientists have discovered over the past twenty years that, in a feedback loop of "amplifying intensity," doing good promotes feeling good and feeling good makes us want to do more good. When we feel good about ourselves, we are more optimistic and have a greater capacity for creative problem-solving and more efficient decision-making, and are more likely to reach out and help others. But it works the other way too. When we do good, we begin to feel better emotionally—more optimistic and hopeful-and physically as well. Our immune systems, instead of being bombarded by stress hormones that can lead to disease (as can happen with negative feelings such as apathy and hopelessness), are bathed in immune-strengthening hormones.

This effect is so powerful that it even works vicariously. An amazing study was done by Harvard researcher David McClelland, who showed a group of students a movie of Mother Teresa working among the poor in Calcutta. Measurements of the students' immune function showed that disease-fighting immunoglobulin A (known to defend against viruses) increased while the film was on and for up to an hour afterward.

This shows that there is a profound connection between being loving, kind, and compassionate and one's mental and physical well-being. And if the research is accurate, the more we are kind to others, the more we will enhance our capacity to think creatively about the problems that we face in today's world.

The amazing thing about this positive feedback loop is that it doesn't matter where you start. Do good and you will begin to feel

better. Feeling better, you will want to participate even more in making a difference in the
world. And your contributions will be
increasingly more useful as your creativity is
engaged, making you feel better and wanting
to do more, ad infinitum. All you have to do
is begin. ❧

## All the Flowers in Our Garden

*"Thank you for being."*

—*TRADITIONAL GREETING OF THE SENECA*

"Nothing, and I mean nothing, can get
under your skin like a two-year-old, and mine
was hyper into outer space. Of course I
wanted to be the perfect parent, but I found
out quickly that my patience was absolutely
no match for the energy level of my son. One
on one we did OK, but when I took him out
in public it was a disaster. I not only wanted
to be the perfect parent, I wanted people to
see me as the perfect parent, and that was
hard to effect when my child was running
amok in the supermarket. So naturally, him

having destroyed my image, I was out to destroy him.

"One day we were in the midst of one of our regular battles in the produce section when he barreled full-on into this older woman. I was mortified, not to mention scared that he had hurt her. That turned out to be a silly fear, because she fielded him like a grounder to shortstop. The next thing I saw was his surprised look, staring back at me from his perch on her hip. For some reason he was so pleased by the whole thing he just sat there smiling while we talked. It turned out she was a mother of six and grandma of sixteen and my dynamo reminded her of her fifth. Caused her no end of trouble until she realized he wasn't trying to be bad, he just had a lot of pent-up energy. So she invented ways for him to burn it off and (thank God!) she shared a number of her secrets with me.

"When she handed me back my perpetual motion machine, she reminded me how important it is to take the time to understand and make room for each of our children's uniqueness, for in our uniqueness our special gifts are found. It was a blessing I will never forget."

The kindness of this stranger, to remind this mother in such a gracious way to appreciate her child, is a gift to us all. For unless we learn to nurture and support the uniqueness of the children in the world, we will continue to be terrorized by the violence and hatred that rejected children let loose in adolescence and adulthood.

As we have seen with the recent horrible schoolyard shootings, our quality of life is directly affected by how well the children around us are raised. Whatever kindness we can extend to children—by being a Big Brother, a supportive soccer coach, a confidante-neighbor—is particularly powerful. For it will ripple out into the world for generations to come. ❧

# Spreading Joy

*The winds of grace are always blowing, but it
is you that must raise your sails.*

—*Rabindranath Tagore*

"El Niño had been hanging around for
months, bringing week after week of gray,
drizzling skies, and it seemed that as every
day went by people got grumpier and
grumpier. Then one day I woke up to bright
sunshine streaming into my bedroom. I don't
know if it was just in comparison to all those
gray days, but it seemed like the light itself
was somehow brighter, as if it had been all
scrubbed and polished by all that rain.

"When I walked out of the house it was
like walking into a populated garden of Eden.
The street trees had exploded in blossom,
flowers were popping up everywhere, and the
air itself was like a delicately scented per-
fume: I floated through that day in a cloud of
joy. What I remember most is that everyone
seemed to be intoxicated. People were smiling to one another, laughing, singing, wav-
ing, skipping down the sidewalk—it was like

someone had dropped happy juice into the city's water supply. We were all reveling in the warm sun and the beautiful flowers."

Every now and then something happens that reminds us not only how crucially important kindness is to our everyday lives, but how incredibly contagious it can be. A break in the weather, a good three-day weekend, the end of a garbage strike, the beginning of the holiday season—whatever the triggering event, suddenly people feel more upbeat, more willing to connect with others. Smiles bubble up to the surface, conversations break out in grocery lines, helping hands are readily extended, and the momentum builds upon itself.

Such times remind us that the ways we are connected are neither mysterious nor inaccessible. They are under our own control and require little effort to put into motion. And, like the small pebble tossed into a still pond, even the smallest effort will ripple out into the world with a wider and wider effect. ❧

# Simple Civility

*Karma is a simple truth:*
*you reap what you sow.*

— WILLIE NELSON

"One year, while visiting an affluent country which will remain nameless, I was shopping in one of the larger department stores when I got forcefully elbowed and squeezed out of the way by several women who were interested in looking over the same sale table I was. There was nothing delicate or accidental about it, and not even a hint of 'Excuse me' in any language. Later, getting on a train, I was similarly pushed and shoved, again without any sign of regret or apology.

"These two experiences were pretty disturbing, but I was really surprised by the negative effect they had on me and how long it took me to get over them. After all, it wasn't as if I got physically injured, but the experience of running into such blatant rudeness completely unsettled me. It was like someone had pulled the rug out from under everything. The more I thought about it, the more

I realized how much we simply expect people to act decently. It seems to me that we all need to keep other people's feelings and needs in mind, and try to be as considerate as possible, as a minimum requirement for a decent day. Without that, every day would be a stress-filled battle zone."

The absence of kindness, of simple civility, not only makes the world an unpleasant place, but can be downright frightening. Imagine what your daily commute would be like if everyone was aggressively ignoring everyone else and just concerned with themselves. It's bad enough when the occasional person cuts someone off and acts like he is the only person on the road or in the subway. The recent outbreak of "road rage" in the United States is not only terribly dangerous to life and limb, but indicative of the breakdown of our sense of civility.

Despite the stresses we each face every day, we can keep kindness and civility toward others in the foreground if we remember the law of karma as articulated by Willie Nelson. When you are about to "lose it" remember that what you do comes back to you. If you are mean and petty, you will get that in return. If you are kind and generous, kindness and generosity will flow your way. ❧

## Beginner's Mind

*Mind is the forerunner of all things.*

—*Buddha*

"I worked for a membership organization that had a pretty large board of directors, and one of the men on the board used to completely bug me. Every board meeting (he was the only board member never to miss a meeting), he'd corner me and start up with his list of ideas. He had ideas for everything, from how to set out materials for board meetings to a host of completely new initiatives he thought we should be investigating. Once he got going, I was stuck for at least a half-hour unless someone rescued me.

"I was never really rude to him, but I came as close as possible without crossing the line, and that use to bug me too. I blamed him for driving me so close to being really rude. One day a friend of mine told me about the Buddhist concept of 'beginners mind,' which is about stripping away all your conditioned responses and trying to listen and react as if this whole experience were something totally new. I doubted it would work with this guy, but I was ready to try anything.

"Next board meeting I was ready. Every time I'd start to get irritated, I'd force myself to stop and wonder why he was saying what he was saying. I'm certainly no expert at it, and I had a hard time keeping it up as he went on, but it was in fact a very different experience, and I discovered at least three things I didn't know before. The first was that a lot of his ideas were actually very well thought out—they weren't always great ideas, but they had a lot of thought behind them; the second was that the seemingly random spewing of ideas wasn't random at all; he'd always start with simple procedural things, then build in abstraction (of course most people never stayed around to hear the big ideas). The last thing I learned was that this beginner's mind thing really helped me stay kind to this man, which I wanted to do, and made me able to sort out what was useful in what he had to say instead of just tuning him out."

Whether you are fighting with your daughter for the forty-seventh time about television, or trying to connect to a difficult coworker over an idea for a project, the experience is made more unpleasant by your annoyed awareness that you've been there before. The very familiarity of the situation, in fact, can numb us to the subtleties of the encounter and the opportunity for a positive outcome. On the other hand, when we have beginner's mind, we come fresh each time to the experience, ready to really hear what he or she has to say because we've never heard it before. Through that openness, something new, does tend to emerge.

Beginner's mind isn't always easy, but it is always useful. Try it today, when you find yourself annoyed at the same old whatever you encounter. It's a kindness to yourself, as well as to the other person. ❧

# The Muscle of Connection

*Do good—to parents, kinfolk, those in need,*
*neighbors who are near, neighbors who are*
*strangers, the companion by your side,*
*the wayfarer you meet.*

*—HOLY QUR'AN*

"When I first moved into my house, an old couple a few houses down went out of their way to welcome me to the neighborhood. They brought over a plate full of freshly baked cookies and a bottle of wine, which we shared while we got acquainted. Over the years we would greet each other, stop to chat every now and then, pick up each other's mail and newspaper when either of us was out of town for a few days, and occasionally get together at a holiday party. We weren't the best of friends, but it felt like we were at least good neighbors. Years passed and one day, I came home to see an ambulance in their driveway. When I went over to see if there was anything I could do, I found out that the wife had had a massive heart attack and died.

"For awhile a lot of us in the neighborhood tried to help out, bringing over food and offering to pick things up at the store, but the poor man was so distraught he was very unresponsive. It was like he went into a cocoon where he didn't even notice the people around him. After saying many 'Good mornings' and not getting a response, and losing a handful of dishes that went in as offerings and never came out again, I gave up. Years later, I bumped into his daughter in the store and found out that he felt like the whole neighborhood had abandoned him. I was astounded and went over to see him when I got home. Sure enough, he couldn't understand what had changed. When I told him everyone just got tired of never getting any response from him, he was surprised. In his grief, he simply not noticed that he had cut himself off completely, while we all assumed it was a conscious decision."

Connection and kindness is like a muscle, it must be exercised to be kept in shape. As soon as we neglect it, we begin to contract away from others and into isolation. Sometimes, in our sadness, depression, or just plain busyness, we don't noticed that we have pulled away. We just wake up one morning feeling all alone. It is then we must get ourselves back into shape by exercising regularly our muscles of smiling, listening, and offering to help. ❧

## Follow Your Passion

*What we love and what captures our curiosity draws us forward into some place of great destiny.*

—*WAYNE MULLER*

"I always though my father was a grumpy (others might even say sour) old man. He was always complaining and had frown lines permanently engraved on his face. When I was still living at home, my sister and I used to go to great lengths to avoid him. He wasn't mean or aggressive, just a giant energy drain that seemed to suck the fun out of life. It never occurred to me there might be an explanation; that was just the way he was and I loved him despite it, but it was sad.

"He worked for a big corporation and took early retirement at fifty-five when his company was going through downsizing and made a special offer to mid-management people. For the first couple months, he drove my mother crazy bouncing around the house like a Ping Pong ball. Then he attended a meeting about restoring a part of an old rural trolley line, and he began to change—he got excited. It turned out my father loved trains, and over the next fifteen years he blossomed into this wonderful eccentric man who couldn't contain his passion for trains. He collected pictures and artifacts from the golden age of the railroad, he built models, tiny models and models big enough for kids to ride on, he opened his own unofficial but wildly popular railroad museum, and—most amazing to me and my sister—he became like the Pied Piper for all the neighborhood kids who couldn't wait to play with his trains and listen to his stories."

When we make plenty of room in our lives for our passions, we bring our own excitement and compassion out into the world.

What excites your curiosity? What engages your passion? It doesn't matter if it is impractical, won't ever make you a cent, is one driving passion or many smaller ones. Finding your passion will make you feel alive and kindly toward those you encounter. And because you are fully alive, people will naturally be drawn to you. ᔈ

## The Strong Embrace of Compassion

*Love and compassion predominate in the world. And this is why unpleasant events are "news"; compassion activities are so much a part of daily life that they are taken for granted and, therefore, largely ignored.*

—*THE DALAI LAMA*

The incredible pace of technological innovation has had a profound impact on our lives, but one area we haven't yet digested is the daily downloading of "news" into our living rooms and bedrooms. It used to be that our daily news gave us all the information we needed, including reports about the bad things that were happening, but the bad-things reports were, for the most part, restricted to local events. Today, every gruesome crime and tragedy from every corner of the world pours out from our television sets every evening. The effect has been to paralyze us with fear. Far too many of us have become convinced that the world is a vicious, cruel, and terrible place that is spinning out of control and that we are powerless to do anything about it.

In fact, there is vastly more kindness and compassion in our world than cruelty and violence, but kindness does not make the nightly news. Boy saves dog is not news; boy blows head off dog is. So we hear about every dog killer and no dog savers. The very process of reporting "news" has created a monster, a shapeless, formless evil that seems to stalk the world.

On the other hand, when we see all this violence and destruction close-up every day on our TV sets, we run the risk of getting "compassion fatigue," no longer caring about the suffering in the world because we have seen it too much. In this way, we can become like Teflon people, horror bouncing off of us without spurring us to responsible action.

The level of evil in the world is nowhere near the monstrous proportions the distorting lens of television would present, but it does exist. We must be willing to face evil head-on if we are to be the compassionate human beings we are capable of being. We need to tune up our own software to keep both our perspective and our compassion alive. ❧

# Commitment of the Heart

*One can only help the sun rise each morning.*

—Joan Baez

The recent murders only two weeks apart in upscale San Francisco suburbs captivated local media. People who had become immune to drug-related homicides in poor neighborhoods were suddenly shocked and scared. Behind the much publicized reaction was the unspoken feeling that some violence was at least understandable, but these murders took place in rich neighborhoods, far from the culture of violence. The implication—that it's somehow OK for poor folks, but not rich ones, to endure violence—is an example of the attitude that keeps us from creating true community. But the point here is that the random nature of these crimes created a feeling of powerlessness, that was even more frightening than the brutality of the crimes themselves.

When we feel like we have been reduced to victims, waiting for terrible things to happen, we usually react by doing exactly the wrong things. We begin to contract. We lose faith in the goodness of people. We lose hope that we will be able to persevere. We cut ourselves off from the one thing that can heal the terrible wounds we are shrinking from—each other.

Once we are made to feel powerless we are already defeated, because the sole source of momentum for positive change is the unrelenting commitment of each human heart to make the world a better place. It is true that we live in a world that we cannot control. Bad things will happen. People we love will get sick and die, accidents will strike close to home, tragedies will occur. Sometime there will be reasons that can comfort us in our grief, and other times there will be none.

These are the things that test our hearts. We can contract in fear, in which case we remove our active compassion from the world and create another opening for evil, or we can accept our grief and fear but remain steadfast in our commitment to live from a place of kindness and forgiveness. It is from these intensely personal decisions that the fate of our world will be decided, because the source of all power is here, in each of our hearts. ❧

## Letting Go of the Trapeze

*The important thing is to be able*
*at any moment to sacrifice what*
*we are for what we could be.*

—CHARLES DUBOIS

"A couple of years ago I watched two very good friends go through a messy divorce. It was difficult for me to navigate through it, since they both were putting pressure on me to be on their side. Each would blame everything on the other person, attribute to them the worst possible motivations, and discount all their good qualities. I couldn't and wouldn't take sides. It just struck me as bizarre that two people who had, in fact, loved each other very well for over ten years had now gravitated to polarized positions, while from my 'neutral' position, I could see that they were basically the same people I'd known for years.

"I know the psychology of a breakup can raise all kinds of demons: feelings of betrayal, abandonment, guilt, resentment, and God knows how many more muddy emotions that make it easy to get angry and stay angry. But what surprised me about my friends was the complete absence of any compassion for one another at all. Each of them was out for blood. Here were two people who under any other circumstances would be wonderfully compassionate and generous, and now neither one of them could squeeze out even an ounce of empathy for the other.

"The declaration of emotional war had stripped them of the capacity to have any concern for each other, and even though they couldn't see it, had dehumanized them both. The hurt, the pain, the mourning—all that made sense, that I could understand—but from where I was, their absence of kindness which grew into a cold meanness was a much greater tragedy."

In any situation, no matter how difficult or painful, we have two choices. We can go into our corner and choose to hold onto anger, resentment, hurt, and fear. Or we can, while acknowledging the hurt we have suffered, open our hearts and look at the other person or situation with understanding, empathy, and forgiveness. In the first case, we end up bitter and contracted, no better and often much worse off than before. In the second case, we end up more wise and loving because we've grown through the experience.

It's like swinging on a trapeze. It feels safe to hold onto the bar we're familiar with. But if we are willing to let go, to swing out into the unknown without a safety net, we find that the new bar is right there beneath our hand. And as a consequence of taking the risk, we end up in a new place. The choice is ours, every time. ❦

# Bless Us All

*Our work-a-day lives are filled with
opportunities to bless others. The power of
a single glance or an encouraging smile
must never be underestimated.*

—G. RICHARD RIEGER

"My freshman year at college was a disaster. I had gone to counselors, read all the materials sent to me by different schools, talked to friends, and I thought I had chosen exactly the right place for me, but when I got there I hated it. I was unhappy from day one. The cloud over my head grew darker and darker and I couldn't shake it no matter what I tried.

"Then one day I was walking along, and as I passed this bench I happened to glance over and see a woman sitting there. In that brief moment of eye contact, she flashed me a smile that was so genuine, so completely real, that it went straight into my heart like a laser beam. I stumbled a little and then started to giggle. I couldn't believe what was happen to me—the walking black hole was smiling! I had been locked into a bad mood for weeks, unable to get myself out of it, and then Pow! like a bolt of lightening I was all lit up like a Christmas tree.

"I found myself wanting to pass that incredible gift along, so I just started being really generous with my smile, and I left a trail of happy people in my wake. That one smile didn't make everything OK, it didn't solve the problem of being in the wrong place, but I found that getting through the days was a whole easier."

One of the most misunderstood forces in the world is the power of kindness. When we think of kindness we think of words like *nice* and *sweet*. In marketing terms it is considered "soft," in politics it is "feel-good." What rarely comes to mind is power. And yet, that is exactly what it is—raw, penetrating, and forceful power. Kindness, the capacity to instantly and effortlessly connect with someone on the deepest possible level, is the single most powerful resource we possess.

What are you going to do with that power today? ❧

# Breeding Kindness

*The gift turned inward, unable to be given,
becomes a heavy burden, even sometimes
a poison. It is as though the flow
of life were backed up.*

—MAY SARTON

"I've been reading some of the excerpts that have surfaced in the press from Ted Kaczynski's journal, and what strikes me most is how normal he sounds. His writing is not like the ranting of a man in a demented murderous rage, which you would expect from the Unabomber, but a kind of understated, unflamboyant, and relatively logical style. Yet, this man sent bombs through the mail to people he had never met. He murdered people and then, writing about it in his journals, treated it like a problem in logistics.

"What is chilling about Kaczynski's words is not so much what is there, but what is missing—any sign whatsoever that this man felt connected to the rest of humanity. It struck me that it was precisely the absence of that sense of connection that opened the gates to unspeakable evil. Undoubtedly Kaczynski's psychological problems are severe, but it wasn't until he withdrew from any contact with others, retreated to his isolated cabin in the hills, that his capacity to do evil actually began to take over."

Kindness is the glue that binds us together as a people, and the absence of kindness opens the gate to otherwise unimaginable horror. Without daily interactions with friends and loved ones, we can lose touch with our moral underpinnings. That's because we each have a gift to deliver to the world—our unique and precious selves—and if we cannot or will not give it, we begin to shrivel and decay.

The single most effective way we can prevent future Unabombers and other kinds of antisocial behavior is to flood our world with kindness. We need to create a community that encompasses and has compassion for even the most marginal members. It is a powerful collective signal, a statement of just how precious we hold human life, that we are willing to spend billions of dollars tracking down violent criminals, doing the police work, investigation, prosecution, and incarceration necessary to stop them from killing again. What we need even more, however, is to pour that same amount of energy into making a society that helps people offer their gifts in a productive rather than destructive manner, a society that breeds kindness instead of killers.

We each have a part to play in this transformation. Take a few minutes today to contemplate what tiny step you and those around you can take to help. ❦

# Stretching Ourselves

*I don't want to get to the end of my life and find that I lived just the length of it. I want to have lived the width of it as well.*

—DIANE ACKERMAN

"I'm the mother of six children, and as they have gotten into high school, they have each chosen to join a foreign exchange program called Amigos. It's a program in which kids from the United States volunteer to spend a month in a Latin American village working on some project—building a sewer or a school, for example.

"As a parent, it's been hard to let fifteen- and sixteen-year-olds go to a developing country, to be on their own in a place where diseases are rampant and they barely speak the language. But I felt it was important not only to expose them to different cultures but to teach them about giving back to the world some of the bounty they have been privileged to receive. As each child would go, it has gotten easier and easier, both for them and for me, for they have all had simply marvelous experiences. While each of them was in a different situation and learned different things, they all came back with a profound respect for the way of life they encountered and a sense that they had received much more than they had given. Said my daughter, 'Mom, these people have nothing, and yet they were so kind to us, making sure we had enough food to eat and didn't feel scared or alone.'"

Isn't this the way it often happens when we set out to do good? When we take the risk to extend ourselves in the world, thinking we are doing someone else a favor, we are rewarded with an outpouring of love and kindness that takes our breath away. When we are willing to live our days to the fullest by reaching out to others, we find our lives infinitely enriched and our souls deeply satisfied.

We don't have to go to Guatemala to find such fulfillment. We can experience it right here—at our neighborhood soup kitchen, at the annual clothing drive for the battered women's shelter, in a Meals on Wheels delivery route. ᴥ

# The Universal Language

*We often visited Ellen's homeland, where our
children had no trouble becoming attached to
the Danish scene. When I asked our son how
he could communicate with the Danish
children with whom he played, he said,
"We can't talk together, but we
can laugh together."*

—Victor Weisskopf

"I grew up deep in the heartland of the
United States and had never even been to New
York when a friend asked me if I wanted to go
to Europe with her. I really wanted to do it. I
had money saved up and knew I could get off
work for the three weeks she was planning,
but I was scared. Just the idea of being in
countries where I didn't know how to talk to
people was unnerving to me. I went back and
forth until the deadline to pay for the airline
tickets, and finally decided that if I didn't go
now, I probably never would and I'd regret it
for a long time.

"That didn't keep me from being nervous.
We landed in Amsterdam, which helped

because so many Dutch people speak English, so by time we got out on the road I had settled down a little. But what I discovered was that for the most part, it hardly mattered at all whether you had a single word in common. If we needed directions we'd approach someone, smile, say "Excuse me," butcher the name of where we were trying to go, wave our hands around and look confused. It always worked! People would smile back, say a whole bunch of things we didn't understand, and then point. Sometimes they'd just grab us by the hands and lead us to our destination."

Kindness is the international language that opens doors anywhere and everywhere. As separated as we are by history, culture, and language, any international traveler can tell you that making contact in foreign countries is an effortless occurrence, and it almost always starts with the universal sign of kindness—a smile—and almost always ends in a laugh.

# 5

# The Transformative
# Nature of Community

*We must accept finite
disappointment, but we must
never lose infinite hope.*

—*MARTIN LUTHER KING, JR.*

The awareness that kindness can realign our lives and build a web of community allows us to see that the evolution of human society is deeply coded into each human heart. We can see that we are a part of a breathtaking process of evolution that has moved human beings from small, insular social groupings based on fear and ignorance to a place where we can imagine an all-inclusive world community that thrives on difference and mutual respect. While the path forward is not easy, it offers an exhilarating view.

Change happens in spurts and leaps, and from all the signs emerging in the world around us, it appears that a very large change is taking place before our very eyes. One consequence of any significant change in any society and culture is that suddenly all the rules change. Things that were once difficult may no longer be problems, and serious new issues may be murky and hard to define.

When living through a period of volatile change, we need to use the power of kindness as well as the nature of change so as to be more helpful and less discouraged. By its nature, social evolution goes through cycles of confusion, struggle, and breakthrough. As we move toward greater community, individual efforts will become increasingly powerful as the massive reservoir of our individual energies merge.

# Visions of the Future

*One's destination is never a place but rather a new way of looking at things.*

—HENRY MILLER

"I grew up in a dysfunctional family. The kind that makes you believe as a child that you won't live to be twenty, and if you somehow did you wouldn't amount to squat. Both my parents were alcoholics, someone was always getting hit, screamed at, or told they were worthless, and we were always moving either because we got kicked out for being disruptive or because my parents hadn't paid the rent.

"My self-confidence was miserable and my picture of what life could be like was limited and dismal. When I was sixteen, my parents ended up out on the street, and the parents of a high-school friend offered to take me in. I lived there for two years, and it saved my life. I was treated with respect, cared for, complimented, and encouraged. The gift those people gave me was the first glimmer of a picture of what my life could be. When I look back now it scares me to think of where I might have ended up without them."

The nature of transformation is that we break through to a newer, more accurate and complete way of seeing. Often we are fortunate, like this woman, to have a clear glimpse of this opportunity when we are still deeply ensnared in the confusion of the moment. It's very much like poking your head out of a thick bank of fog that has obscured your vision for a long time and seeing the clear light of day. This is not to say that this woman won't have a hard road ahead, but she has been given a vision of a better life.

As our consciousness evolves, break-throughs occur regularly. They are welcome moments of clarity before we sink back down into the fog of our daily lives and must work our way out again.

In your life, what issues of connection are you are struggling with? Forgiveness of a family member? The desire for a loving extended family? A neighborhood in which people have regular get-togethers and are there for one another through thick and thin?

An office that feels nurturing and supportive? Where have you been shown a vision of what might make your dream come true? ❧

## Part of a Great Whole

*Sometimes I go about with pity for myself and all the while Great Winds are carrying me across the sky.*

—OJIBWAY SAYING

"Since I've been a voter, the person I've voted for has always lost. You could predict the outcome of an election by it. It didn't matter whether it was for president, Congress, statewide office, or even local—my choice always went down in flames. In a similar way, at any social gathering where any topic of controversy arose, I was always the underdog and ended up surrounded by upset people who couldn't believe what I was saying. It makes me sound like a member of some fringe cult or political group, but I'm not. I'm a child of the sixties, and in a way most of my adult life I have missed the feeling of belonging that I remember from that time.

"Recently my candidates have started winning elections here and there, and I find myself not so outnumbered anymore. A few months ago a doctor friend was going to a conference on mind/body healing, and since it was in a beautiful spot, I tagged along for a mini-vacation. I was really taken aback by the collection of people that showed up. I felt more like I belonged in that group than in any group in years, and my knowledge of how the human body works is about as basic as you can get. Either I'm starting to think like everyone else or they've all been in hiding for thirty years and are just surfacing."

Some fascinating demographic studies recently shed light on this phenomenon. What the studies demonstrate is that the social, political, and cultural character of the United States is changing rapidly, and that the changes are being driven by the generation of people who grew up in the sixties. This should not be too surprising, since the baby boomers have always been the single largest demographic bulge in the population, and it makes sense that the changes they are initiating are reflective of their values. This demographic group, labeled Cultural Creatives by Paul Ray, who did the ten-year study, is made up of people of all ages who support environmentalism, feminism, and voluntary simplicity. They believe in the importance of community and relationship, downplay financial success, are idealistic and altruistic, and reject hedonism, materialism, and cynicism. What is surprising is that Ray discovered that despite the size and growing momentum of this group (currently about one-third of the population), the individuals within it all tend to think they are alone, or at least in a distinct minority, in their beliefs and attitudes.

This is a snapshot of social change, which you might want to nail on the wall to remember on days you feel frustrated and isolated. You are not alone, and soon, very soon, we will be faced with issues of efficiently and effectively managing the growing momentum for change. ❧

# We Are Today's Leaders

*Vision is not enough, it must be combined
with venture. It is not enough to stare up
the steps, we must step up the stairs.*

—VÁCLAV HAVEL

The deaths, within days of each other, of
Princess Diana and Mother Teresa are a powerful metaphor for our time. These women
shared an extraordinary capacity to captivate
us while representing the best parts of our
humanity. They were in most ways complete
opposites: Diana the statuesque, beautiful
princess, who lived surrounded by luxury;
Mother Teresa the tiny, unimposing, no-non-
sense older woman, who before Diana had
even been born had already spent a lifetime in
the slums of Calcutta working among the
"unwanted, unloved, and uncared for."

Although Diana was in the spotlight
because she was a princess, she moved us so
deeply because she represented the best part,
the truest part, of all of us—the imperfect,
flawed, vulnerable person who just wanted to
do the right thing. Conversely, Mother Teresa,

a commoner, became true royalty in our eyes. Clothed in the garb of the poor, she embodied the very best of humanity.

The very fact of their existence gave us hope. They reminded us that we are all in this together; that we are all, from the poorest resident of Calcutta to the inhabitants of Buckingham Palace, connected in this incredible experience of life. They reminded us of the enormous power of love and kindness. They helped us to believe that we could live in a world where compassion and love mean more than wealth and fame. And, to our shame, we all too often simply allowed them to carry that burden for us.

When they died, the whispered question was, "Who will replace these two extraordinary women?" The answer is that no one can, and all of us must. Our job now is to hold onto that truth and start acting on it. The time when we could wait for our heroes to do good deeds is over. Mother Teresa and Princess Diana have left the stage, and it is time for the rest of us to step forward. ❧

# Be Prepared!

*We should be encouraged by historical
examples of social change, by how
surprising changes take place suddenly when
you least expect it, not because of a miracle
from on high, but because people have
labored patiently for some time.*

—HOWARD ZINN

Social change has a pace and trajectory somewhat akin to a roller coaster. First there's a long, slow, torturous climb up an endless hill, when nothing seems to be happening and it takes enormous energy just to keep going. Then the cars finally reach the crest and plunge with death-defying speed down the other side, follow a series of rapid twists and turns, little hills and sharp drops, and then begin a new ascent.

Human history has taken thousands of rides on this roller coaster, each one bigger and faster than the last as the rate of our population growth and the momentum of our history accelerate to breakneck speeds. We are now perched at the very top of the biggest roller coaster ever, and the first couple of cars are already peaking over the edge. From this vantage point we see glimpses not only of the quality but also of the sheer scope of the changes that are about to come rushing upon us: the destruction of the Berlin Wall and the collapse of the Iron Curtain; the end of apartheid in South Africa; efforts toward peace in the Middle East and Ireland. All are movements away from fragmentation and disconnection.

One particularly striking event that may not make it into history books but is powerfully reflective of the character of the emerging changes was the outpouring of grief in Britain at the death of Princess Diana. Diana was a symbol to the British people of a new kind of royalty—one who ruled over a kingdom of kindness and compassion, where people stumbled and made mistakes but never lost their empathetic connection to one another. Her role was deeply honored when this nation of stiff upper lips and tightly controlled emotions broke out in a cathartic period of public mourning. It's indicative of the worldwide desire, despite our differences, to treat one another with love and caring.

Change is moving with incredible momentum and leverage. Things that seem impossible or at least improbable today will unfold with blinding speed tomorrow. Exactly what the changes will be we can't say. What we can do is keep the faith and not let what seem to be problems deter us from adding our efforts on a day-to-day basis. We need to watch out for every possible opportunity for nudging, pushing, and encouraging positive change. Even though it may seem today to be an impossible task, at some point it will unfold with blinding speed. ∿

# Seeds of Community

*We are all part of the earth and it is part*
*of us. The perfumed flowers are our sisters;*
*the deer, the horse, the great eagle, these are*
*our brothers. The rocky crests, the juices of the*
*meadows, the body heat of the pony, and*
*man—all belong to the same family.*

—CHIEF SEATTLE

"I was visiting a friend, and while we were sitting there chatting away, the doorbell rang. She got up to answer it and came back carrying a large box full of fruit and vegetables, with a big smile on her face. She told me it was her weekly delivery from her organic produce service. The service was organized by a collection of local farmers and for a regular, and very reasonable fee, once a week they would deliver to your door a box of locally grown organic produce. The selection is entirely dependent on what's in season.

"What a great idea! Not only do you support local farmers, but you get organic produce, which means that you are eating more healthily and not contributing so much to water, soil, and air pollution. In addition, it eliminates a lot of excess packaging found in most supermarket chains, and, in it's own fashion it reestablishes a more personal and direct relationship to the food you eat. I loved the idea but my critical side had to have its say-so. I asked, 'What if I don't like this week's selection?' My friend laughed and said she had the same thought in the beginning. One of the more interesting features of the service is that it breaks you out of your culinary habits and stretches your imagination. You could fax the service a list of 'never sends,' of things you absolutely hated. The service also produced a newsletter in which subscribers could share ideas, recipes, and stories. I signed right up. It's a way for me to live my commitment to environmentalism and good health."

Opportunities for community-building are cropping up everywhere, often in unexpected ways. We need to keep our eyes open for the possibilities sprouting up around us. ❧

# Connection Not Consumption

*We make a living by what we get, but
we make a life by what we give.*

—Norman MacEswan

"I always thought high school reunions
were strange and never bothered to show up
until my twentieth. Even then, I only went
because I had already committed to be in
town that same weekend for my parents' fifti-
eth wedding anniversary. It *was* strange, but
not in the way I had imagined. Seeing all
these people I had known as youthful and
unformed, now smack dab in the middle of
their lives, was a shock to my system.

"I was a very successful financial analyst, a
bit on the driven side, but it got me all the
things I thought I wanted—a great co-op
apartment downtown, country house, fancy
car, classy clothes. So I showed up with a bit
of a self-satisfied attitude. There were plenty
of surprises, both in appearance—it is amazing how many different ways there are to
age—and in what people have done with
their lives. The biggest surprise to me was that

the people who really seemed happy with their lives were not the people who had 'made it' in the sense I would have understood. There was a pretty good-sized handful of people in my economic bracket—doctors, lawyers, a few corporate bigs—but for the most part they were the least interesting and least happy group at the reunion.

"The interaction that knocked me off my tracks was with an old girlfriend, and not because of any rekindled love, although it did make me remember why I had liked her. She was a schoolteacher and when she talked about her job, her 'kids,' and some of the things she was doing in her classes, her eyes would light up with a kind of excitement and energy that I hadn't seen for years.

"It came to me that she had a very deep connection to the people around her, whereas I had all the trimmings of a great life but it wasn't connected to anything. That was the beginning of my midlife crisis, and I'll be honest, it has put me through the wringer. But it also feels like I am awake again after years of sleepwalking."

Each of us has only a finite amount of energy, and where we put that energy reveals our values, what's important to us. When we put our energy into acquiring things like a large house, fancy car, or a wad of savings for retirement, we reveal that objects are more important to us than people. We don't consciously think we're doing this, but take a minute to reflect on it: Are you so caught up in the rat race that you have little time for the intangibles that makes your heart sing and gives your life its most meaning—a walk in the park with a friend, attending your son's soccer game, a call to your widowed mother to tell her you love her?

How we spend our time is how we spend our life. ❧

# Nurture Your Dreams

*Dreams are the seedlings of realities.*

—JAMES ALLEN

"Since I was young, I have always had a deep longing to live in community with other people. Somehow the conventional two or three people in a living space just never made sense to me, both in terms of wasting resources (do we all need hammers and washing machines and refrigerators?) and the burdens it places on the members to be the be-all and end-all for one another. In college and beyond, I tried several varieties of communal living situations, which, because we were all young and inexperienced in group dynamics, were failures of one sort or another. Since then, I've lived in a conventional household, with my husband and kids, but in the back of my mind I never gave up the dream of somehow, someday, finding a group living situation that worked. But I couldn't figure out how to make it happen.

"Recently my husband and I decided that we needed to downsize—we just weren't making it financially—and began looking for a smaller house. We searched for months, but nothing seemed right. It was really hard for us to give up our dream house and move down. Then we came across a house that had a smaller cottage in the back of the yard. Focused on the finances, we decided to buy it because the rent from the cottage would make the mortgage manageable. It wasn't until weeks later, when one of the women who was going to move into the cottage offered us her pick-up truck to use in renovations, that I realized that this living situation could offer what I'd been looking for all these years: pooled resources and good people to connect with. I wasn't consciously setting out to do that, but somehow it just happened. If anyone told me my money troubles would have resulted in my dream coming true, I never would have believed it."

We all need dreams to carry us forward into the future. Author Dawna Markova says that when we put out into the world what we want and set our intention on it despite all the obstacles we "know" are in our way, there's like a giant rubber band between us and the thing we want, propelling us toward it, often, as in the case of the woman in this story, without our consciously trying.

Take a moment right now to reflect on your dreams. Do you harbor a secret wish to join the Peace Corps? Move to a small community where everyone knows your name? Have more time to spend with loved ones? Don't worry about how it can possibly happen. Just envision your dream, set your intention, and go on with your life, open to whatever may help you realize your dream, no matter what form it takes. ❧

## Savor All Paths to Connection

*"Men work together," I told him from the heart, Whether they work together or apart.*

—ROBERT FROST

"I grew up with computers and have always been Net-savvy, so of course I had e-mail before it came into its own and was a big advocate of the online community. For four years of my life I probably spent as much time online as off, and there are still things about it I think are really great. The scope of people you can interact with is breathtaking, many more than you could ever hook up with in physical space. Also, because you are anonymous, you have the opportunity to open up quickly to total strangers.

"At the same time, I know that for some people the anonymity leads to inflated imagination and lying. Some of that does take place, particularly in the boy-girl chat rooms, but for the most part I never found that to be a problem. Most e-inflation is pretty obvious.

"What made me cut back my involvement was that I finally concluded that the online community lacks depth. Maybe because of vast number of people you can communicate with, most e-communications are just dabbling. A little chit chat, back-and-forth questions and answers about incredibly superficial and meaningless things and then Poof!, people disappear.

"It amazes me how often and suddenly people just drop out of sight. You think there is something real going on, and then complete silence, like it never even existed. No explanations, no good-byes, just silence. The more I checked in with friends, the more I had to conclude this was the main mode of e-communications—a brief flurry of e-mails and I-mails going back and forth, the illusion of connection, and then a trickling away."

There is an old saying that nothing is overvalued as much as something new. The vastly overhyped "solution to all problems" Internet offers the latest proof of that statement. In any process of change, all the pieces will shift, sometimes in quality, sometimes quantity. We should expect the same for emerging ways of connection. Perhaps the Internet is, for some folks, a true virtual community, and perhaps over time more of us will learn how to connect via computer in satisfying ways. Or perhaps the Internet is just a temporary way-station on the path to something else.

We don't need to take sides, but we should experiment and be curious about any kinds of connection that can foster a sense of community. ❧

# Coming Together Regularly

*Commitment is the love that*
*binds energy and desire.*

—ANONYMOUS

"It seems like the world really has sped up, and the accelerating spin of the planet is pushing all of us further and further apart. I have fantastic memories of family gatherings with all my aunts and uncles chattering away and doing delicious things with food, while all of the cousins were engaged in some high-energy activity. We were a sporting family, so a lot of my memories were of volleyball or soccer on the beach, occasional get-togethers with baseball games taking over the suburban street where my aunt lived and then, of course, the big football game on Thanksgiving.

"As we grew up the get-togethers changed and then dwindled. I still saw my aunts and uncles occasionally and my cousins less often, since we had all dispersed around the country, but for all practical purposes we were barely hanging on as an extended family. It is easy enough to explain: we all have our own lives and our own circles of friends, and in truth most of what connects us is in the past, but the older I get the more I realize how important our pasts are and how much those people and connections from our pasts are a part of who we are.

"So it was with great pleasure that I received a beautifully decorated invitation to the all-new annual family golf tournament and dinner, and it was even more satisfying when the entire family showed up. That was three years ago and we are still going strong."

So much can get in the way of our being with those we care about. Instead of just bemoaning that fact, why not take the bull by the horns and make something happen? If you live far apart, make it something do-able—plan a year in advance for some inexpensive location. It doesn't matter if every single person can't show up. Try for something that a good number of you can do, and make it a regular occurrence: a Fourth of July barbecue; a family trip to the lake for a week-end. Rotate so that one person doesn't have the whole burden or organizing it every year.

Whether with family or friends, extended time together is a vital part of being alive and feeling a part of something greater than yourself. As the commercial says, "Just do it." ❧

## Cashing In on Community

*Infinite riches are all around you if you will open your mental eyes and behold the treasure house of infinity within you.*

—*JOSEPH MURPHY*

It started in 1991, during a serious economic recession in Ithaca, New York. Some local people were bothered by what they saw as "poaching" by national chain stores that would come in, drive local businesses out of business, and then ship all the financial gains back out to national headquarters. The Ithacans decided to mint a local currency, Ithaca dollars, which have a value of one hour of work or $10 in U.S. currency. Ithaca dollars could only be spent in Ithaca, on Ithaca businesses. Today, Ithaca dollars are widely accepted by markets, restaurants, taxis, medical clinics, and a host of service providers like lawyers, repair people, painters, electricians, babysitters, and house cleaners.

The idea caught on not only in Ithaca, but has spread to over forty other communities. It makes a commitment to local businesses and the local community by keeping money in circulation that might otherwise leave town. It has also resulted in some interesting side effects—a local currency can build a sense of community pride and connection. Ithaca merchants who accept the currency report that they prefer the Ithaca dollars, because each transaction is not just an exchange of currency but an act of faith in the long-term sustainability and value of the community. Even the bills themselves reflect this feeling: emblazoned on the front is the slogan "In Ithaca We Trust."

Your community doesn't have to print its own currency but, like the citizens of Ithaca, we can be creative about the ways we show support and commitment to the people who live and work in our community. ❧

# We Are Not Our Wounds

*The times do not allow anyone the luxury*
*of waiting around for others to lead. All have*
*leadership charisma to offer the community*
*and ought to be invited to do so.*

—*MATTHEW FOX*

"I got married right out of high school, and two children and five years later it was over. I guess we were too young to get married and expect anything to come of it, and I know we were too young to get divorced properly. There were a lot of nasty recriminations, and the bottom line is that I got cut off from my children for nearly ten years. During that time, I got to thinking of my life as a series of disasters that needed to be overcome.

"I finally went to therapy and began to figure a few things out. It never seriously occurred to me that my own parents' angry battles might have had any influence on my life. After a while, I felt like I was beginning to get things back under control and worked up the courage to try to reconnect with my children. I had a speech all practiced about how sorry I was, how much I missed them, and would they please let me back in their lives. When I finally saw them, I never got it all out; I broke down and they both hugged me.

"That first day we talked about a lot of things, but what keeps coming back to me was how they looked at me as if I were something special. There I was feeling like one giant wounded man, and they just saw me as their dad, finally come back."

When we are cut off from the ones we love, it's easy to define ourselves solely by our wounds, by all the ways we have been hurt and maligned. Without strong connections and input from others, we become isolated, and in our isolation the places that hurt, the places that are raw and bleeding, capture our interest. Conversely, the more we are connected to loved ones and are engaged within community, the more we are defined not by what we are lacking but by our presence and our impact on the lives of those around us. There is a time for introspection and healing, but there is also a time to offer our gifts to others; otherwise we become lost in our wounds. ❦

# Abandon Self-Limiting Views

*We all have the extraordinary coded within
us ... waiting to be released.*

—*JEAN HOUSTON*

"When I was young, I was a terrible student. It was an excruciating experience for me because my parents were both college-educated and expected a lot from me, but things just didn't make sense to me no matter how hard I tried. The irony is that I tried really hard. I was so ashamed of how poorly I did in school; I used to sneak school books into my bed at night with a flashlight to try and make sense of them.

"Somewhere along the line my parents quit pushing and I resigned myself to being the dumb guy. I barely made it through high school, compensating by playing sports with a vengeance, even getting good enough at baseball to attract some minor league interest. But I knew I was not big league material, so I went to work right out of high school and did construction work for six years.

"Then I married a very bright woman who

had the good sense to disagree when I told her I wasn't academically inclined. After I tried to go back to junior college, we discovered that I was seriously dyslexic. A little training later I was on my way. In five years I had a master's degree and now teach at a junior college. I love my work so much that my wife jokes she should have never pushed me to get tested, since she sees less of me now then she did when I was working construction."

One of the most common ways we sabotage our own growth is by building up self-limiting views of our lives: I can't do that; I'm not smart enough for this; not rich enough to try that; too old; too shy, and so on, endlessly. When we don't push beyond our limiting ideas of ourselves, we never grow into the exceptional, extraordinary human beings we have the potential to be.

The same mechanism operates with community. Looking out at our social landscape, it's hard to imagine how this fast-paced, very materialistic and self-absorbed society could ever evolve any real forms of community. This just points out why something new and different is needed. Society is a collection of individuals. We need to go beyond our self-limiting ideas and focus on doing our part to reach out to others, and trust that the extraordinary potential of the whole will emerge. ❦

# Searching for Signs

*Great things are done by people who think*
*great thoughts and then go out into the world*
*to make their dreams come true.*

—*ERNEST HOLMES*

It is easy to look out at our conflict-ridden world and despair, but we need to hold on to the true harbingers of the future, the places where the strength of the human heart is asserting itself on the world stage. When a massive earthquake devastated the city of Kobe, Japan, aid poured in from all over the world. When Hurricanes Hugo and Andrew tore through parts of the South and the Caribbean, assistance came from around the world. Tornadoes in Nashville and Alabama, floods in North Dakota, China, and Italy, drought in Malaysia, fires in Florida and Mexico, starvation in war-torn Sudan, refugees in Rwanda and Bosnia—natural and manmade disasters around the world regularly result in increasingly organized and significant international aid.

On an institutional level, the United Nations

and governments worldwide have begun to see international relief as their normal responsibility rather than as an extraordinary emergency effort, or as just an adjunct to good diplomacy. Organizations such as the International Red Cross and Red Crescent Association have grown dramatically in size, scope, and influence as the compassion of the world's people has escalated. Just as the increasing speed, penetration, and concentration of the news media has dramatically increased our awareness of disasters everywhere, so too have people responded out of a powerful sense of empathy that crosses national boundaries.

Never before in human history has so much energy, so much attention, been focused on trying to help others. Natural disasters will come and go, but in the emergence of planet-wide responsibility for each other, we are seeing an evolutionary development of tremendous significance. Don't be misled and disheartened by the loud noises and bright flashes of tonight's news; look deeply at the ways behavior is changing and the ways people are changing their thinking. ❧

# Humanity over Politics

*I can honestly say that I was never
affected by the question of the success of
an undertaking. If it felt it was the right
thing to do, I was for it regardless of
the possible outcome.*

—*GOLDA MEIR*

It started in 1991 as a simple conviction
born of bitter experience. The Vietnam
Veterans of America Foundation decided that
enough was enough—land mines had to go.
The Veterans marshaled the gruesome evidence of the devastation such mines can cause
long after a war is over, and began to network
with organizations around the world. By
1997, they had built an international movement of over 1,000 organizations and had
succeeded beyond imagination, with virtually
every country in the world (except, ironically,
the United States) signing on to a complete
ban on land mines. As an acknowledgment of
their efforts, the international umbrella organization and Jody Williams, the woman who
spearheaded the movement for the Vietnam

Veterans of America Foundation, were jointly awarded the Nobel Peace Prize in 1997.

Forget for a moment the shameful resistance of the United States, and think about what has happened here. The rules of warfare, long the jealously guarded domain of the military powers of the world and their sovereign governments, have been rewritten by an international mass movement of individuals. Ordinary people, from almost every country in the world, banned together to say: This is wrong, this perpetrates brutal, cruel, and unjust treatment of the people of the world, and it must be stopped. *And it was!*

This is an extraordinary achievement, not just for what it accomplished but for the precedent it has established. The network built by this movement represents a powerful and truly international community—people from nations strewn with land mines, people from countries that profit from the manufacture of land mines, and people from countries with no interest whatsoever in land mines other than the conviction that they are morally reprehensible. All these people from different and different cultures came together to force the world's governments onto a more humane and compassionate path.

When the linked voices of people from every country in the world have the power to dictate the terms of our future, we have cause to be hopeful. We live in extraordinary times. ❧

# 6

# Experiencing the Kind Caress of Community

*The least of things with a meaning is worth more in life than the greatest of things without it.*

—CARL JUNG

At one time or another, all of us have experienced the kind caress of a sense of community. The simplest one can take place at any time—a moment of true connection with a stranger. Each of us has stories of times when we were in need and a total stranger came through for us. The quality and texture of that experience is breathtaking in its depth and importance; sometimes it even alters the direction of a life.

Conversely, the experience of extending your hand to a stranger in need usually does not carry such dramatic impact. Being the bestower of kindness has its own character, a deeper and more subtle sense of correctness, as if in that moment you simply know that this is how you want to live your life.

Occasionally the delicious sensation of being a part of a larger community will take us by surprise. We may feel it in a comedy club where the audience has been drawn together in laughter; in a sports stadium during an exciting game; listening to a live performance of powerfully moving music; in a conversation with three other people in the office about a new direction for the company. It can come over us any time a common thread of energy weaves us together with others to share, if only briefly, the experience of truly experiencing something together. For that moment, we are carried away on the crest of a feeling we recognize instantly but share far too infrequently. Such events, as well as the memories of powerful connections we shared living with others, usually in our early adulthood, in college, and beyond, remain as reminders of what is possible.

As we grow older, as we begin to realize how much our inner focus has isolated us, we are drawn to rediscover new, healthy ways to connect with others. To do so we must let down the guards many of us have built around our hearts. But we can do it. We can learn not to fear letting others inside our defenses. We can cultivate the capacity to make more and more room for others in the deep recesses of our hearts. We learn to forgive what once seemed unforgivable transgressions, and in our daily interactions we can accumulate more and more moments of real connection.

# The Whole World Is Home

*One never reaches home, but wherever friendly paths intersect, the whole world looks like home for a time.*

—Hermann Hesse

"I was standing on a dock in southern Spain, looking down at the tugboat that was supposed to be my passage to the Canary Islands. As far as I knew the only cargo besides myself was a Land Rover taking up the whole deck, and a couple of members of Generalissimo Franco's police force who were escorting four surly looking criminals to the prison on one of the islands. It was not looking like a promising two-and-a-half days. As we started to board, one more passenger appeared, looking for all the world like a scruffy friend of the prisoners. My imagination went into overdrive, with fantasies of jailbreaks and murder on the high seas. I almost jumped ship.

"Fortunately I didn't. After a bit of delicate spy work, I discovered the latest arrival was a Canadian named Louis who lived in Paris and who had nothing in common with the hand-cuffed cons, other than a few scars and a fair coating of road dirt. As soon as we sailed out of the harbor it started raining and didn't stop. Louis and I set ourselves up in the Land Rover and talked our way across the choppy sea. After just a few short hours, it felt like he had been my closest friend for years. We talked, we laughed, we talked some more, and then we laughed some more.

"That was thirty years ago, and even though he lives on a different continent and we only see each other every three or four years, our connection is always effortless and completely real. Meeting Louis was my first evidence that it is possible for people who don't know each other well not only to get along, but to take true delight in one another's company. It was that immediate and undeniable connection that opened my eyes to the possibility of a real community of humankind."

Immediate, close bonding between two people is a miraculous gift, one that most of us have had the honor and joy to experience.

Today, take a minute to bring to mind the face of someone you have felt this way about. Would a phone call to them right now feel good? ❧

## Nature's Guide

*Earth teach me to remember kindness
as dry fields weep with rain.*

—Ute prayer

"I had been working a pretty crazy schedule for about two months, when my sweetheart announced we were heading out to a cabin she had rented for the weekend. It was a unilateral, no-argument statement that would usually have prompted an indignant response, but I was sane enough to recognize (after working four straight weekends) that I had no firm ground to stand on. I went, but with misgivings, since the sad truth was I still had a ton of work to get finished.

"The drive up was a little strained and our first evening unfolded stiffly, not at all what she had planned, but I was having trouble changing gears. The next morning, I decided to get up early and take a long run in the hills to try to loosen up. The morning mist was just beginning to burn off, and by the time I had gotten a few miles up the trail, the entire valley just opened up to the stunning beauty of a mid-autumn day. The air had an incredibly fresh pine fragrance to it, the play of sharply outlined shadows as the morning sun filtered through the trees was almost a living thing, and the sounds of the waking forest were a well-orchestrated symphony. It was so beautiful I stopped running and just tried to become a part of it for a while.

"When I got back to the cabin, I felt like everything was beautiful and wonderful. Sure my work still needed to get done, but suddenly it was so clearly not worth turning myself into a maniac about."

The downside of our capacity to think and abstract is that we can easily think ourselves into a knot that is a universe away from what is important. Sometimes we need the widest and most primal approach that only nature can provide to bring us back to solid ground.

Throughout most of our history, we have lived deeply connected to the world around us, but that awareness has been severely strained over the last hundred years. Finding ways to rebuild and honor that connection can give us the solid foundation we need to come back to ourselves, and to one another. Make a date to wander in nature sometime soon and see what that does for your interactions with others. ❧

## The Right Thing

*Cultivate the giving habit as you*
*do the saving habit.*

—*Grenville Kleiser*

"It had been one of those days when absolutely nothing went right. I woke up half an hour past my usual time to stare dumbly at the digital clock blinking at me; the electricity had gone off, then back on sometime during the night. I started late and never caught up—my computer kept crashing on me, I got copy machine toner all over my shirt, a client had a screaming fight with one of my assistants who threatened to quit if I didn't back her up, and when I finally got to my car to make my escape it looked like a flight of pigeons had hovered over it.

"Needless to say I was frazzled on the drive home. After I finally got out of the city, I saw a car on the side of the interstate with an old man staring under the hood at a fountain of steam. He looked even more dejected than I felt, and I guess that was why I pulled over. He'd been having problems for weeks with a slipping fan belt and he thought he'd fixed it by replacing the belt, but apparently he hadn't put it on properly because it was gone and the radiator was boiling over.

"I drove him up to the next gas station where he picked up a new fan belt, then drove back, put the belt on his car and showed him how to tighten it properly. By then his car had cooled down enough to start up. He thanked me and we parted ways.

"A few miles later, I realized I was singing along with the radio and feeling remarkably good. The thought struck me that I should have been the one to thank that old guy. Taking the time to lend him a hand had acted like a reset button on my mood."

Helping someone in need is not only a "nice" thing to do for others, it rewards us with a sensation of correctness, like this is the way we should feel all the time. Lending a hand pulls us back from our preoccupation with ourselves and lends a nice sense of perspective to our days. Make a pledge to do one random act of kindness a day and see what happens. ❧

## From Need to Joy

*Magnanimity is the expansion of the soul to great things. . . . [It] strengthens a person to take on good tasks.*

—Thomas Aquinas

"Some years ago I lived in a two-story apartment building that had one stairway for each of four units which shared a small balcony. I was working part-time and going to school part-time. Next door was Sara, an intern with a schedule that had her coming and going at all hours; across the hall was Maria, a single mother of two who worked at the department store; and John, an older guy on disability. The truth is we had very little in common, very different backgrounds, cultural roots, and ages, but we shared a balcony and a group of schedules that made life difficult at times.

"I think our getting together started with a plea for help from Sara. She needed someone to let the repairman in to replace the broken hot water heater in her unit, and for the next two weeks she was on duty at the hospital from sunrise to sunset. John took the morning shift and I picked up the afternoon when I came home to study. One thing led to another and we gradually learned to depend on each other for a whole host of things, from baby-sitting, grocery shopping, and laundry to rides and car repair.

"Somewhere along the line we started congregating on the balcony on Friday evenings in the summer for a few drinks and unwinding, and that shifted to more sporadic but still regular indoor morning coffee sessions during the winter. Through it all we became a pretty close group and we definitely knew we could count on one another. Gradually our own lives took us in different directions, and I rarely see any of them anymore. Sometimes I feel guilty about that, but then I really think that while we were once almost a team, our purpose was that of mutually supporting each other through a difficult time, and now we are all living different lives. I still cherish the open generosity and easy way we shared with each other."

Often we are pulled into making connections with others by need, and then discover the bounty of that bond. But as this woman notes, circumstances change, and just because you no longer have that connection doesn't mean that it was meaningless. Instead, we can use those memories to remind ourselves to open to others in whatever situation we find ourselves. What will give us the joy and comfort of being nestled in a community without impinging on our need for personal time and space? How can we recreate, in ways and forms that fit into our current needs, the feeling of closeness we may have experienced in the past? ᴖ

## Communities That Work

*Do what you can with what you have, wherever you are.*

—Theodore Roosevelt

"I've worked at a lot of places, but in retrospect one job I had for a few years really stands out, not for the money or even the challenge of what we were doing (it was a public relations firm dealing with high-tech companies) but for the incredible camaraderie that developed among the 'junior' people in the office. We were all relatively new hires and all around thirty, and we just hit it off fabulously. Coming to work was fun, people covered for each other, made each other laugh, comforted each other when it was time to cry, put up with meltdowns and tantrums, stood behind each other when the senior staff got uppity, and just generally bonded like best buddies at summer camp.

"It lasted in full force for almost two years, and by the end included regular get-togethers, Thursday night dinners, pooling of shopping and dry cleaning runs, and even some double-dating. Then it wound down as people moved on to other jobs and other cities. That was six years ago, and it still brings a smile to my face when I think about it. I don't know if that was a really unique experience or not, but I miss it. We spend so much of our time at work it seems to me there should be a way to create at least some of that caring and fun at almost any workplace."

For most of us, a high priority is restructuring or repositioning our workplace so that it can provide us with some of the traditional benefits of a community. That means breaking down all the artificial hierarchical structures and prohibitions that squeeze the life out of employees, and inviting the whole person (or at least most of the person) to come to work.

For those lucky enough to have found great colleagues, celebrate those connections and give some thought to how you can bring those experiences into other parts of your life. If you long for such bonds, what can you do to create them? Bring in bagels and have a pre-work coffee klatch? Invite everyone to a weekend movie? ❧

## Investing in Community

*Give humanity hope and it will dare and suf-*
*fer joyfully, not counting the cost—hope with*
*laughter on her banner and on her face*
*the fresh beauty of morning.*

—John Elof Boodin

It's easy to feel so overwhelmed by a problem that you are paralyzed and can't do anything. Imagine how Mohammed Yunus must have felt, wandering through the streets of Bangladesh in the mid-seventies, surrounded by crushing poverty and famine. But doing nothing wasn't an option for him, so he did something he knew would help at least some people—he lent some extremely poor people a very small amount of money. They used that money to buy materials for small cottage-industry businesses, and then they paid the loans back.

What started out of frustration turned into the Grameen Bank, which by the mid-nineties has already made over 2 million "micro-loans," and has not only become the source of pride and hope to millions of people in Bangladesh, but has created a world-wide micro-loan movement that is rewriting many of the old, staid ideas about banking and economic growth. It is a great irony, after the savings and loan fiasco in the United States and the banking scandal that triggered the economic downturn in Asia, that the professional bankers of the world, the same people who scoffed at the very idea of lending poor people money, used such poor judgment when lending money, while the Grameen Bank, lending to the poorest of the world's poor, has a 98 percent repayment rate.

Through the efforts of the Grameen Bank, economists are finding that micro-lending is astonishingly efficient at building sound, local, self-sustaining economies. It is a return to what banks were originally supposed to do—pool a community's wealth so that those in need can draw on its strengths.

Mohammed Yunus' story shows how a very small action, taken from the heart, can grow over time into a groundswell of positive change. Yunus reminds us that our actions, no matter how small and seemingly ineffective, can potentially have powerful consequences. ᴥ

## Oh, Holy Night!

*It is up to you to illumine the earth.*

—Philippe Vensier

"A couple weeks before Christmas, I flew to New York to spend a week with my sister. In the late afternoon I arrived at the airport, where she picked me up. We stopped in the city for an early dinner before heading to her house. On the way there, she asked me if I wanted to take a slight detour and do the "annual Christmas tour." Actually, I didn't, I was ready to get to home base, unpack my bags, and put my feet up, but I said yes. The tour turned out to be a slow drive through the five or six blocks around her house. Everyone had done things up as festive as possible, with sleds, Santas, and reindeer on lawns and roofs, elaborate nativity scenes, snowmen, Wise Men, bright colored lights everywhere including around the stop signs, and roving bands of people wandering the streets and singing Christmas carols.

"Coming from a suburb where you can't even tell if anyone has a Christmas tree, it was a visual treat not to be believed. When we finally cruised into her driveway, I was the first to suggest we head back out on foot. It was a wonderful and almost magical experience. I counted four different groups of carolers. Occasionally a couple of them would meet up, and they'd join together for a few carols and then split up again.

"The highlight of my trip was this evening wandering through the neighborhood, looking at the lights, listening to the music, greeting and being greeted by the crowds of admirers. For that brief time, I could almost imagine that we were in a small village, and not a suburb of New York, that these were all our friends and neighbors, and that everything was right with the world. It was hard to return to our private enclave in Southern California."

We rarely think about it, but the ways that we can interact with others are almost limitless. In this spontaneous winter wonderland, the neighbors created something that went well beyond the decorations. They created a collective sense of place, a feeling of peace, joy, and celebration, a welcoming and comforting atmosphere that held the power not only to raise holiday spirits, but to remind us of the importance of our lives together. A neighborhood Thanksgiving barbecue, a community Fourth of July celebration—we need to be conscious of those opportunities when they arise and seize them with both hands. Community is not an intellectual exercise, it is a deep resonant feeling. ❧

# The Art of Community

*Our brightest blazes of gladness are
commonly kindled by unexpected sparks.*

—Samuel Johnson

"When I was a kid my parents forced me to take violin lessons. I hated it and dropped it as soon as I could. Thirty years later, I was a hard-core classical music listener (who wished he had stuck with the violin) at a music festival in Vienna. I was in heaven. Music in the parks every day, more music than you could possible get to scattered around at the city's music halls in the evening, and even an occasional string quartet set in a music room of an old Hapsburg palace.

"Vienna in the summer is a classical music lovers' paradise, and it didn't matter one bit that I couldn't speak a word of German; the music is its own language. One evening I sat next to a well-dressed elderly gentleman through an incredible performance of Beethoven's Ninth Symphony. When it was over, I was surprised to find myself applauding with tears streaming from my eyes and even more surprised when I turned to my side and saw my well-dressed neighbor in a similar state.

"He looked at me, smiled, shook his head in disbelief, and just applauded louder. I never found out where he was from. I assumed he was Austrian, but I realized later that, for all I knew, he could have been a neighbor of mine in Chicago. All that mattered was that we shared something amazing, the recognition and acknowledgment of a kind of human beauty that crosses all boundaries and calls out to our souls."

The traditional foundations of community are place and need, usually in combination; we are thrown together and rely upon each other for support. But the deeper threads that tie us all together go well beyond the limits of our neighborhood and even our needs. They are the subject of art: music, literature, painting, design, dance, and cinema, all the varied ways we try to capture the mystery of our existence. What is so powerful about art in all its forms is a profound paradox: each piece is a uniquely individual expression that somehow taps into a powerful universal feeling. In artistic expression, we come closest to be being both unique and universal at the same time. As such, it should be a model for community. ❧

## Risk Reaching Out

*Don't be afraid to go out on a limb;*
*that's where the fruit is.*

—*Anonymous*

"A while ago I read an article about an Amazonian tribe that had emerged from deep hiding to enter into dialogue with the outside world in the hope of protecting their rapidly shrinking world from destruction. It was a fascinating story, but what captured my attention was an interesting habit of the tribe—they shared their dreams with one another. Much of their culture is built around a belief that the dream state is an important communication from another realm, so it was important that they all know what was being dreamed. Each morning they would gather to go over what each member of the tribe had dreamed about the night before. Tribal decisions were never taken without first allowing time to dream about the options. Even the courageous and very radical step of reaching out to the modern world was prompted by dreams."

Imagine if the first thing we did upon arriving at work in the morning was to stop by the conference room and share our dreams with our fellow workers. Or classes at school began with a brief review of the dreams of the night before? Or couples and families shared dreams upon waking and never made decisions without consulting their dreams? What would emerge? Would we learn anything useful about ourselves? About our world? More important, what effect would it have on our relationship to our fellow workers, students, family members?

It's not likely that in our society, where privacy is so highly valued, that the widespread sharing of dreams would ever occur, but what other forms of connecting communications already exist or may emerge? If we want in our lives a healthy balance between our need for individuality and our need to be a part of a larger community, then we need to recognize that at the moment we are seriously out of balance. We must begin taking risks as individuals in order to feel a part of something larger than ourselves. We must start somewhere. Perhaps that means sharing your dreams with a close friend, or joining that support group you've been afraid to go to. ❧

## Expanding from Love

*The love of humanity is the natural outgrowth of a love for a single individual. From one man to all men.*

—Leo Buscaglia

One of the few places in our lives that we have experienced the extraordinary potential of community is in our romantic relationships. Certainly, these relationships are not always easy, not always joyful and satisfying, but at the very least, within them, most of us have experienced times of profound communion. Moments, days, even weeks, when we have felt known, accepted, and cherished, when we didn't have to pretend to be someone other than who we are, when just being ourselves brought us into magical synch with another human being.

Given the tumultuous state of our most significant relationships today, it appears that maintaining that state of communal grace is not a simply thing. Ironically, the pressure that we put on our significant others to satisfy completely our need for deep connection may partly be the undoing of so many relationships. The powerful combination of the need for human companionship, coupled with sexual desire, gives us courage to take the risks that are necessary to expose ourselves to another and to get to know another intimately. Then, having tasted the exquisite fruit of that close bonding, we simply assume it is the only place we can ever have that experience.

We may have focused, with destructive laser-like intensity, all of our needs for community on our most significant relationships. The result undermines our romantic relationships, because no one person can satisfy our hunger for community. It also distracts us from important lessons we can learn about the nature of all loving connections, not just romantic ones: the greater the personal risks we take, the greater the potential return; the more of ourselves we offer to others, the better the chance for deep connections; in love we expand outward to others and in fear we contract back into ourselves.

Our deepest adult connections with "the chosen one" can be a learning experience for our continued growth as a communal being. We can grow from that delicious embrace, by courageously and deliberately moving outward to expand the circle of people who can and will support us, accept us, and love us for who we are. ❧

# 7

# Only Kindness Allows for Community

Compassion allows us to bear witness
to suffering, whether it is in ourselves
or others, without fear; it allows us to
name injustice without hesitation,
to act strongly, with all the
skill at our disposal.

—SHARON SALZBERG

On the other side of our deep longing for community is our desire to have everything just the way we want it, with no compromise and negotiating. At bottom, this represents a complex intolerance of difference in a world of stunning breadth and diversity. If everyone were exactly the same, we would not have any trouble getting together. We would agree on everything.

The world doesn't work that way, fortunately, and it is the bumping together of our differences that gives life its spark and allows the new to emerge. However, in our struggle to become clear about who we are and what we need, we tend to have less tolerance for those who are different from us, and less time for those outside our sphere of interest. We want to be a part of a community, but summoning up the tolerance to deal with others on anything but the most superficial level can seem an overwhelming task. Our intolerance can lead to a lot of suffering—for ourselves and for those we are judging.

This "narrowing" of focus is not all bad. To accomplish anything, we need to make choices; to stand for something, we need to make judgments; and to be truly who we are, we need to respect our priorities. The danger is when we go beyond personal preferences to judgment (not "I am different," but "I am better"), beyond principled stance to personal dismissal (not "I believe in this," but "What you believe in is irrelevant"), beyond attention to our own priorities to active disregard for others (not "How I feel matters," but "I don't care how you feel").

Nothing tests us quite so completely as another human being, particularly one who is very different from us; and, by definition, the more deeply we expand our experience of community, the more "others" will test our patience and our limits. An essential ingredient, if we are going to make it through, is a healthy dose of kindness and compassion for our own flawed stumbling.

## Appreciating the Odd Man

*To understand another human being you must gain some insight into the conditions which made him what he is.*

—MARGARET BOURKE-WHITE

"The last three years I was in college I lived in a fraternity. Everyone at the house was involved in sports including Stan. Stan was a swimmer, but all I remember was that he was a source of constant friction at the house. No matter what anyone wanted to do, Stan would always come up with an objection. By our senior year, some of the younger brothers couldn't figure out why Stan had been allowed to pledge in the first place. It wouldn't have been so bad if he had realized he was the odd man out and just kept his mouth shut. But Stan took his being a brother seriously, more seriously than anyone else, and his constant pointing out of the rules and regulations drove everyone crazy.

"I ran into Stan in New York a while back when I was helping to chaperone a group of high school honor students on a field trip to the United Nations. It turned out that Stan was working at the U. N. on international relief issues, and gave the kids a great insider's view of how things worked. We got together later and spent a great evening together reminiscing and updating each other on our mutual friends.

"I'd had a few drinks, and I asked him why he had always been such a pain back at the frat. His answer was that we were all such a collection of unthinking jocks, he used to go out of his way to be contrary just to get us riled up in the hope of producing some minimal amount of actual thought. I told him I didn't think it worked, we just thought he was there to irritate us, and we both had a good laugh.

"As we spoke more, I realized that he was a deeply sensitive person, dedicated to making the world a better place, and none of us had been aware of that side of him while we were living together. His parents had instilled in him a strong sense of obligation to serve others, and he had a hard time with the 'party hardy,' self-involved atmosphere of the fraternity. I realized that I had more in common with him than with some of the guys I had always considered my closest friends, and we have continued to stay in touch."

In every group—office, family, civic organization—there tends to be at least one person who represents, if only silently, the minority perspective. It's easy to dismiss that person, thinking that they are crazy or disruptive, or irrelevant. But almost always he or she has something important to contribute that is being ignored. Part of working together well is understanding and honoring the outsider's contribution and finding a way to incorporate, rather than dismiss, their concerns into the activities of the whole. Can you think of a situation right now where this is going on in your life? Perhaps you are the outsider.... ❧

# Welcome Difference

*There is nowhere you can go and only be
with people who are like you.*

—Bernice Johnson Reagon

"I was part of a weekly women's group a few years ago. I had joined at the invitation of a friend and for the first year I really enjoyed it. Our group had nine women in it, and getting to know them all, listening to their stories, and telling my story to a sympathetic group was wonderful. I learned a lot in that time, particularly about how similar and how incredibly different we can be. What really struck me was that from the outside we looked like we had very similar lives and concerns, but once people started talking about the details of their lives, while there were plenty of 'Oh, yeah, I've been there' comments, for the most part we were very different people. After the first year, our differences started to surface in funny ways.

"One woman got upset any time one of us said anything positive about men. Another woman didn't want to talk about anything but men. Then there was a running eight weeks where we alternately discussed and avoided discussing the merits and dangers of stay-at-home mothering (four stay-at-home moms and four working moms and one working undecided) and each of us had a hard time not judging those on the 'other side' of the issue.

"Eventually, the group got focused on self-esteem, and that's when I started to lose interest. It's not that I don't think it's important, it's just that for one reason or another, self-esteem has never been an issue for me. In retrospect I didn't exactly take my leave properly, but I was still surprised at the vehement reaction I got from some of the women. I started missing sessions fairly regularly and then apparently was obviously bored when I did show up, and at my last meeting, I got jumped on by four of the women. They said I was insensitive and uncaring, and a few other not terribly nice things. It both surprised and hurt me that they could turn on me so quickly, but clearly I had suddenly gone from being one of them to being potentially harmful.

"After the attack stopped stinging, I realized that I had been pushed away because they felt vulnerable. My good sense of self-esteem was something they wanted, and yet they were angry that I didn't suffer the way they did. For my part, I realized I should have been a lot more straightforward and found a way to move on without having to force a confrontation."

There is no "good" or "bad" in being different; there is just difference. But we are so conditioned to seeing situations and people as "us" and "them" that it is difficult in a group to accept our differences in a gracious manner. In this group, for instance, perhaps the woman telling the story could have helped the group work through the issues around self-esteem, or the working and nonworking mothers could have found ways to support one another. When we truly welcome the teachings that come from diversity, we are all enriched. ❧

# Equal Doesn't Mean the Same

*The most terrifying thing is to
accept oneself completely.*

—CARL JUNG

"In the early seventies, I worked for a
weekly newspaper that was owned and operated by the employees. In most ways it was a
great place to work, except that it took its phi-
losophy a bit too seriously at times. We started
from an admirable position of wanting to
treat everyone equally, with respect and consideration for their desires as well as their
abilities. That got translated into an credo of
'Everyone is equal,' which then turned into a
job-rotation system in which we literally
switched jobs every six months.

"Thinking back, it is amazing we stayed in
business. In a lot of ways it was great fun, and
we certainly got a taste of what it was like to
do every job, as ad sales people became writers, writers did production, editors filled
news racks, and designers edited. Six months
later we all switched again to yet another new
set of tasks.

"We learned a hard lesson: We may all be equal in the ultimate sense of our worth and value as people, but we sure weren't equal at doing any given task. It sounds downright silly now, but in the midst of our idealism, it came as a surprise to us that people who were good designers couldn't necessarily string two paragraphs together, people who were good writers couldn't sell water to a man dying of thirst, and our best ad salesperson couldn't put an ad together that didn't tilt to the right. We had to face that each of us had unique talents to contribute, and they were all different."

In some ways, as obvious as it seems, we make this mistake all the time. How many times have we been annoyed at someone who is not as organized as we are, or as punctual, or as articulate, or able to fix the machines that break around us? We get annoyed because we expect that they should be good at the same things we are.

It's a paradox, but the more we accept ourselves as exactly the way we are, with our strengths and limitations, our foibles and our talents, the more we can accept others exactly as they are. It is only when we try to deny either our gifts or our weaknesses that we insist on a false democracy where everyone should be exactly the same. This can be scary, as Carl Jung has noted. It requires a ruthless self evaluation—What am I good at? Where do I flounder?—and then an outpouring of self-love for both the good and the bad. Honor yourself for the totally unique human being that you are, and you will smile in appreciation at the totally unique others you encounter on your path. ❧

## Be Responsible for What You See

*One bad apple can spoil the whole barrel.*

—AMERICAN PROVERB

"A few years back, I was involved in an environmental group that had a full-time staff of around ten people and ten or so regular volunteers. It was a great group of people, but there was one staffer, who happened to be a wizard at fund-raising, who took so much of everyone's energy it got exhausting. He had a very strong personality and insisted on being the center of attention. He wasn't mean, but he was far from a model of psychological health: he couldn't deal with any criticism without becoming incredibly defensive; he was blatantly (to everyone else) manipulative; he would talk behind people's backs, half the time making things up completely; and if anyone ever tried to call him on it he'd go into the injured innocent mode and generally cause all work to stop while we dealt with his 'crisis.'

"The sad thing is that he got away with it. Most people were too scared to say anything since he would instantly turn it into a huge battle; some people felt we should learn how to put up with other people's dysfunctions; and the handful of people strong enough to stand up to him were afraid of being blamed for driving out the fund-raising guru. This went on for a few years, and while the fund-raising was pretty successful, the organization began to turn sour from the inside. People lost their enthusiasm and eventually their desire to make the sacrifices they had to make to work there. It didn't end until a couple of staff people finally just had enough and refused to put up with him any more. Of course it resulted in an ugly battle and the departure of the fund-raiser."

In any group setting, we owe it to the group to be responsible for not only our own behavior, but for the behavior of others who are adversely affecting the group. That doesn't necessarily mean major confrontations, and it doesn't mean the absence of flexibility and tolerance for individual quirks, but it does mean making basic respect for the individuals in the group a bottom-line requirement for participation. It is not OK to turn away and hope someone else with deal with it. We must learn to deal with one another squarely, honestly, and yet respectfully. ❧

# Speak the Truth Kindly

*What we nurture in ourselves will grow;*
*that is nature's eternal law.*

—ANONYMOUS

"My wife and I were stuck in a very awkward place and no matter what we did we couldn't seem to get out of it. On the surface, the conflict was about a commitment my wife had made to me and to herself about getting back into law practice after our youngest child had reached a certain age. That was three years ago, and not only was nothing happening, but every attempt on my part to remind her turned into a fight. I was getting increasingly upset and impatient, and she was digging in her heels more and more.

"At that time our oldest child was going through the obnoxious teenage years of 'I'm right,' 'You don't know what you're talking about,' and 'That's stupid.' He was so rude that I sat him down and explained that you just can't say things like that even if you are right; you have to be sensitive about what other people are feeling. As soon as I said it (he wasn't listening anyway), a crisp clear bell went off in my head, and I realized I'd been doing the exact same thing, only on a much more subtle level, with my wife. Sure, I was right, and she was avoiding even talking about the issue, but that was not what was important. That evening we had a wonderful and tearful journey through our fears and uncertainties; and sitting in the kitchen at two o'clock in the morning, giddy with ourselves for finally breaking through, we raised a toast to our son to thank him for reminding us that just because something is true, you don't have the right to say it sharply."

Being in community with even one other person requires us to learn new skills or remember old ones. One such skill is the ability to speak our truth in such a way that other people can hear it and feel able to speak theirs. In an argumentative culture, full of put-downs, sarcasm, and yelling, it can be very challenging to speak kindly, especially when in conflict. But if we are to relate to one another in positive, healthy ways, we need to practice speaking kindly. The more we practice, the easier it will be.

One way to practice is to take a deep breath before you are about to blurt something out, and ask three questions: One, Is this true? Two, Is this useful? Three, Is this kind? Only if you can answer yes to all three questions do you then speak. ❧

## Participate Gently

*In the beginner's mind there are many possibilities. In the expert's mind, very few.*
—SHUNRYU SUZUKI

"For some years I was involved with a community group that was trying to revitalize part of an old downtown residential neighborhood. The purpose was great, the plan was solid, and the enthusiasm of people living in the neighborhood, as well as the merchants we were courting to come back into the neighborhood, was high. It should have been a wonderful experience, particularly since we were successful in the long run, but the truth is it was a very unpleasant experience. The main reason was the behavior of one person, the man who started the organization in the first place.

"He was not a bad person, he just carried around a big basket full of personal issues and seemed completely unaware about the effect he was having on other people. We would be in meetings, and if anyone said anything that he disagreed with, look out! The lowest level of response was a scowl, a very big, totally undisguised scowl. From the scowl it went to a disgusted shaking of the head and from there to his interrupting to tell you were 'totally wrong.' Sometimes, in his more subtle moods, he would resort to his litany of 'credentials' ranging from 'being the only one here who was brought up in this neighborhood,' to the ever-successful 'I started this group for a reason.'

"I honestly believe it was not his intention to destroy meaningful discussion and run roughshod over the group, but that is the effect he had. He was so offensive that at times you just wanted to argue with him, even if he was right. Of course when the project took off, he assumed the credit was due to him, and the irony is that it worked despite him, and everyone else knew it."

In any group situation, there are people of very different dispositions. All too often, in the absence of sound and sensitive leadership, the more powerful and assertive personalities tend to dominate. That can be a barrier not only to the achievement of the desired results, but to the creation of a true sense of community participation as well. When those assertive individuals are unconsciously using the group arena to play out their own issues, it can completely undermine any sense of group identity unless the problem is dealt with effectively.

Fortunately there are a number of group dynamic techniques that can be employed to make sure that one person doesn't dominate the group. One of the most useful is the concept of council, best illustrated by the Native American council scenes in the film *Dances with Wolves*. In council, everyone who wishes to speak is heard, with no comments by others allowed. When you speak, you speak your own truth, not a response to what someone else has said. To learn more about this and other useful community techniques, see the book *Call to Connection* by Carole Kammen and Jodi Gold ❧.


## The Harsh Mirror of Community

*The seat of a soul is not inside a person or outside a person but the very place they overlap and meet with the world.*

—*GERARD DE NERVAL*

"I had done a lot of things in my life and have always been a pretty sociable guy, so after my wife died, after four years of bouncing off the walls in the home we had lived in for thirty years, I was intrigued by the concept of shared housing. One of the things that really attracted me was the idea of living with people of different ages. I might be sixty years old, but I still enjoyed being around younger people, particularly children. Plus, being older and better settled, I could bring not only some economic resources but also a degree of maturity that seemed to me would be a real plus in making it work.

"I started attending meetings of a local group and eventually ended up in a group that included a young family with two small children, a middle-aged couple without children, and myself. The process we decided on was very energizing and a lot of fun, although it was challenging at the same time. Trying to balance all our interests and budgets into a plan that worked wasn't easy, but eventually the happy day came and we moved in together. By then it seemed we had already been through so much together that actually living together would be a snap. The big surprise to me was how quickly I gravitated to serious grumpy irritation. I have always been a fastidious person, and I guess I just forgot that not everyone likes their glasses lined up and their refrigerator carefully segregated. Within a month I found myself muttering to myself and getting upset over the stupidest little things, just because they weren't the way I wanted them to be, and I thought I was the mature one. I realized I had a long way to go to be the kind of person I imagined I was."

When we open the door to living within a broader community, we also open the door to the hidden recesses of our own process. Issues that rarely arose in the privacy of our personal lives, issues we had become adept at sidestepping, or those we thought we had dealt with suddenly emerge in glaring detail. It can be a shock to find yourself staring in the mirror at behavior that is far below your well-established personal standards. At times like this, you need to accept your failing with grace and compassion and at the same time appreciate the rare gift you have been offered of a clear reflection into your soul. ❧

# Working through Anger

*Being angry isn't destroying others,
it's destroying yourself.*

—Yoko Ono

"I worked for a while as a political consultant, and during that time I became friends with John. He was a big cocky Irish guy who loved the excitement and gamesmanship of politics, and just knew he could find a way to have a real positive effect. He worked as a lobbyist for a high-powered organization, and after four years of very effective work, he got set up by a small group within the organization and was fired.

"John didn't take it well; in fact he got furiously angry and obsessed with showing them what idiots they were and single-handedly undermining their legislative program. He started doing contract work and had no trouble getting clients, but he would devote more and more time to screwing up his old employer than to his new clients. On top of that, he wasn't much fun to be around since all he wanted to do was curse these guys out and talk about how he was going to get back at them. At one point, I told him I thought he should just let it go and get on with doing things he wanted to do. His reaction wasn't printable, and that was the last time I ever saw him.

"I lost track of him almost eight years ago, but recently ran into his now ex-wife who said he was a completely unhappy, bitter man who drank too much and didn't give a damn about anything or anybody. As far as I can tell, he never realized that he kept right on giving those jerks that fired him more and more power over his life by becoming so focused on his own anger and desire for revenge that he essentially gave up everything else."

Anger is a poison that, left untreated, has the capacity to destroy the very closeness we seek from our family, friends, and coworkers. Is there someone you have a grudge against? What kind of healing do you need to leave the grudge behind? ❧

# Forgive, Not Forget

*To forgive our brother is to*
*forgive ourselves. . . .*

—LE LY HAYSLIP

"Years ago, I worked on a project with a group of people and, as often happens, we ended up in two factions. Because I was romantically involved with the leader of one faction, I held a grudge for years against the other group for the way they treated my boyfriend. As time went on, he didn't seem to care, but I did. I even refused to attend a reunion of the group twenty years later because I was still mad. My friends said I missed out on a wonderful time, that it was really great to see everyone and discuss how they'd grown over the years."

As many spiritual teachers have pointed out, forgiveness is something we do more for ourselves than for the person we forgive. Grudges create separation—between us and the people we are angry with, and, more important, between ourselves and love. If we can't let go of past hurts, we can't be fully in the present, ready to connect with those who are holding out their hands to us. Without forgiveness, we cannot have community.

If you have been wounded, you may need to make a promise to yourself, some kind of boundary that you can use to protect yourself, before you can forgive and move on. A promise to listen to your intuition, or to take care of your needs, or to speak up if you are hurt. Only you know what promise will help you feel safe enough to connect again.

That being done, it's much easier to forgive because you know that you won't betray yourself. You might try this prayer by Levi Yitchgak of Beditschev: "Lord of the World, I stand before you and before my neighbors—pardoning, forgiving, struggling to be open to all who have hurt and angered me. Be this hurt of body or soul, of honor or property, whether they were forced to hurt me or did so willingly, whether by accident or intent, whether by word or by deed—I forgive them because we are human. . . . I am ready to take upon myself the commandment, Love your neighbor as yourself." ❧

# Overcoming the Wear and Tear

*We have come . . . into that more difficult*
*time when it is a person's duty to understand*
*the world rather than just fight for it.*

—*ERNEST HEMINGWAY*

"I attended a reunion for environmental and peace activists whom I hadn't seen in almost twenty years, and was pleased to see how much we had all managed to grow up. A recurring theme in most of our discussions was the burnout phenomenon—these were all people who were deeply committed to what they were doing, but every one of them at some point had pulled back into a very private existence, sometimes for many years, before reemerging and getting involved in group activities again. Most of us were young when we became activists and were suffering from the affliction of most twenty—some-things—we thought we knew everything so a lot of the wear-and-tear of those years was self-inflicted.

"I had an hilarious talk with a man who had been a close friend at the time and who recounted with amazing accuracy some of the ego-trips and guilt-trips that were a frequent part of our organizing days. He told this great story about a meeting where one of the leaders of the growing women's movement lit into him personally for oppressing women for 2,000 years! That story made us laugh hysterically, partly at the image of this poor twenty-year-old boy standing accused of centuries of crimes, but also because we had all been hurt a lot more than we ever were willing to admit at the time."

The tendency, rising largely out of youth and immaturity, to take the blows, stuff away the hurt, and go on led many of us later to pull away completely, so that we wouldn't have to deal with people and the hurt that they could inflict. We need to find ways to protect ourselves from these pitfalls of group dynamics. This will become easier as more people take responsibility for healthy group interactions. We also need to build downtime into our lives, so that we can have solitude without feeling overcome with guilt.

Take a moment today to think of the interactions that regularly irritate you, or the kinds of behavior that make you want to recoil. Are there things you can do to avoid these situations? Is there something you can kindly request of others that will make the situation easier, for example: "If you have something difficult to convey to me, please do it in a note and not verbally," "I would appreciate it if you would start with something positive before making a critical comment," and so on? Rather than just suffering in silence and then withdrawing, we need to request that others treat us the way we would like. ❧

# 8

# The Practice of Community

*Practice makes perfect.*

*—PROVERB*

Building community takes practice. When we become aware of our own longing to be a part of a larger community, it can be a life-changing breakthrough that throws open the door of possibilities. The experience can be so powerful that it may fool us into believing that the open door is enough, that having arrived at the threshold with an open heart and a willing spirit, the rest will simply unfold.

The reality is wholly different. Most of us come to the realization that communicating well with even one person—a good friend, a lover, a spouse—can be extremely difficult. The opportunities for misunderstandings, for scraping against sore points, or simply encountering an out-of-sorts moment are plentiful.

With our loved ones, we struggle through the mess and are better for it. When we extend ourselves out into our communities (many of whose members we don't know intimately), the opportunities for misunderstanding increase dramatically. Suddenly the path to community resembles a run through an obstacle course rather than a walk down the yellow brick road. We need to proceed with caution, knowing that we will stumble and fall, that we may unwittingly find ourselves embroiled in disputes we neither invited nor wanted.

We will need to back up, regroup, try again, and in the process learn to do it better the next time. The old rules may not always apply terribly well. When we got together with our extended family, we all knew not to tease Uncle Bert about his job, exactly how to avoid irritating Aunt Sally, and so on. The building of broader communities is considerably more challenging, because the rules and traditions for doing so do not yet exist.

What protocols do you follow when you have little in the way of shared history? Where are the boundaries, and how do we even begin to discuss how to make these decisions? Like the pioneers of earlier centuries, we can only find the solutions by doing and learning. We can take a look at attitudes and behaviors that may help us in this new terrain.

# A New Way of
# Listening and Seeing

*When love listens, it listens with an ear
and a heart to the unspoken.*

—DAPHNE ROSE KINGMA

In the West, we have been well trained in observation and analysis. We collect facts like seashells, line them up neatly in rows, and bring them out to support our ideas or opinions. This system of observable and measurable results underlies most of our scientific and technological advances. It serves us well in most cases, but now we need to develop a new kind of observation to supplement our logic: a kind of perception that allows us to look at shapes and texture; to feel movement, desire, and the energetic threads of life that pulse all around us; to hear how people's discussions are changing;  and to see not only what is on the surface but what is just under the surface.

If we are to be the midwives of a new world based on kindness, compassion, and inclusiveness, then we need to practice seeing and hearing what's missing, what's struggling to emerge. We do this not just by peering into shadows (although much can be seen there) but by putting aside analysis for a moment and allowing ourselves simply to listen, observe, and wonder. Resisting the urge quickly to categorize everything we see and hear, we need to ask questions about why something is there is the first place, and if there is anything behind it that could be of interest.

At first, this can be very difficult to do. The temptation, when fed new information at work, in discussions with friends, and even with loved ones, is to rush in with our thoughts and opinions with barely a breath's interval. We need to slow down enough to give space for new thoughts and perspectives to form, to truly hear what others are thinking and wondering about, and to give ourselves the time, figuratively, to try on a new set of glasses. Once we begin to do this we are quickly rewarded. What we begin to see is not a "better" vision of the world, simply a more complete one, with a richness and texture that is reward in itself.

In a Buddhist meditation group we know, people take turns speaking, and before they begin and when they are finished, they bow slightly from the waist, and everyone else bows back in response. It may feel awkward in the beginning, but this practice is helpful in two ways: first, it honors both the speaker and the listeners, acknowledging the important role of all parties in an encounter. Second, it slows the whole process down, both the speaking and the responding, so that there is deeper listening, and deeper thinking.

Other groups use a talking stick, rock, or shell. If you are holding it, you can speak. If not, you must remain silent. This, too, helps slow things down and allows time for those who need to get their thoughts out without interruption. Both techniques work as well in heated family conversations—say between a parent and child—as in a larger group. ❧

# Visualize Community

*Just as despair can come to one only from
other human beings, hope too can be given to
one only by other human beings.*

—ELIE WIESEL

"I was once told a story about a woman who grew up in an old neighborhood on the East Coast and returned many years later to find it had gone the way of many inner-city areas. The sight of the broken windows, boarded-up buildings, and trash on the sidewalks distressed her so much she couldn't get it out of her mind. The neighborhood she remembered was old but beautiful, so she decided to do something about it. She bought a falling-apart corner building and, with the help of friends, fixed it up into a small market with her living quarters on the second floor. When she opened for business, people from the neighborhood drifted in to see what she was up to. She found out years later people had been suspicious, since no one had tried to do anything nice in so long they figured there must be a trick.

"Her first year in business wasn't terribly successful, but customers began to show up, and she started to develop a reputation for having good produce at reasonable prices. But she had an ongoing problem with shoplifting. Instead of installing cameras or other security systems, she turned the front corner of the market into a small café where she served coffee, tea, and inexpensive pastries, and she set up a planter box outside the store filled with brightly colored flowers. Gradually she attracted a set of regulars, her café was occupied most of the day, and her shoplifting problem disappeared.

"Years later, her market had become a prized anchor in the neighborhood, and as she continued to spruce it up, adding a few outside tables in the summer, more flowers, and a new colorful paint job, the rest of the street began to catch up with street cleaning, repairs, and a few new shops opening. It is still a very poor neighborhood, but a neighborhood with its own beautiful center and measure of local pride.

"What struck me about this story was this

woman's ability to see not what was there, but what could be there, and then to act with great determination on her vision without letting the always-present obstacles deter her."

When you look around where you work or live, do you have a vision for improving your office or neighborhood? It doesn't need to be as ambitious as this woman's. Perhaps a community garden in the vacant lot, or a flower bed in the office parking lot. Visualize what you want and then enlist others to help ❧

## Give Up Expecting Instant Results

*The only way things will happen is if people get over the notion that they must see immediate success. If they get over that notion and persist, then they will see things happen before they even realize it.*

—HOWARD ZINN

Because our reliance on the environment is so enormous, environmental issues have become a bellwether of our progress toward a broader definition of community. After all, with our environment each of us holds responsibility not only for the people alive today but for future generations as well. Environmental issues ask us to think about community in the widest terms possible: not only the human community, but every strand of the great web of life: oceans and air; winged, furred, and scaled creatures of all sizes; mosses and trees and minerals and rivers.

When evidence first appeared that our use of fluorocarbons was destroying the ozone layer, people around the world began demanding an instant halt to the use of the offending chemicals. After years of effort and grassroots pressure, an international treaty, which satisfied almost no one, was signed. (Environmentalists insisted it was far too tentative, while industry representatives criticized it as unnecessary and too expensive.) Now, years later, a new report shows that for the first time since we began monitoring the ozone layer, the rate of depletion has slowed instead of growing. This is hardly a stunning victory for the environment (global warming is increasing so fast that even scientists who have been skeptical for years have now agreed that it is occurring), but it does demonstrate something crucially important: In a world of people who will argue and disagree about just about anything, positive change can take place. It just usually takes a lot of pressure and patience to see it through.

That does not mean that each of us shouldn't do everything possible to move change at the quickest pace possible (environmental issues in particular are increasingly urgent). But if we don't get instant cooperation from everyone, we should not become so frustrated that our own efforts become derailed. ❧

## Have Faith in Momentum

*The drop of water is only weak when it is removed from the ocean.*

—*BAIRD T. SPAULDING*

"I attended a talk back in the sixties by an exiled sociologist from South Africa about the problems in his home country. He painted a very real and depressing picture of a country completely torn apart by racism and hatred, a country where it seemed impossible to imagine any change. The white rulers were certainly a minority, but they were a very large minority that held all the power, while the black majority was beset by tribal differences and weighed down by poverty. Then, at the end of his speech, he talked for a while about this guy, Nelson Mandela, who had been imprisoned for organizing against apartheid. I remember thinking, in my youthful arrogance, how terribly heroic and yet totally futile Mandela's efforts must be. Mandela's release, the end of apartheid, his election as president—all of these changes have given me such hope."

Change can be painfully slow, particularly in the beginning. It takes tremendous energy to get a large boulder moving, and then eventually less and less energy produces greater and greater movement. The initial inertia that must be overcome in our efforts to make the world a better, kinder place is overwhelming, and often it appears as if nothing is happening at all. At times like that we need to keep doing the things that need to be done, even if they don't appear to be having any effect, and trust that every little nudge will impart some energy that will eventually achieve a cumulative momentum.

If we look hard at the world around us, the beginnings of that momentum are plain to see: the crumbling of the Cold War and defusion of ideological differences, increasing government sensitivity to environmental issues, global concern over wages and working conditions, increased grassroots activity in local communities. There are already hundreds of thousands if not millions of people around the world pondering the same questions and ready and willing to lend their shoulders to the effort. Bringing all those pieces together will take time and hard work, but the boulder is already moving. Our job is simply to increase its momentum. ❧

## Start at the Beginning

*The time is always right to do what is right.*
—*Martin Luther King, Jr.*

"My husband and I recently let a young woman, the daughter of a friend, stay at our house for a few weeks. We really like her, but as time wore on, we were put off by the fact that in the whole time she was there, she never offered to cook or clean or in any way contribute to the collective effort of making our household tick. After thinking it over, we finally concluded that at heart she was a very sweet and good person. She simply didn't know what the appropriate behavior would have been. Her way of showing her closeness was to treat us like her parents (who strayed a bit too much on the serving side of things)."

We as a society are a lot like that young woman when it comes to social behavior and community values—we haven't been trained well, and all too often we don't have a clue what we should be doing. It isn't that our hearts are in the wrong place, it is just that we have no model, no training, and no tradition for being in a close and supportive community. Much of our history in the last hundred years has been about the breaking down of traditional communities, as we have moved away from family and isolated ourselves more and more in housing built for privacy rather than communion.

Our behavior has giant holes in it and can leave us feeling helpless. We rally when a crisis strikes, but are overwhelmed to inactivity by the weight of chronic problems like homelessness, and we never see the subtler signs of need and distress. Before we can practice being good community-builders, we need to retrain ourselves to pay attention to the plight of others, to develop good sensors that alert us to the stresses around us so that we might act to relieve them. We do this through a commitment to acts of kindness in our day-to-day lives, whenever the opportunity arises, and by encouraging them in our children. ❧

# Becoming Second Nature

*Replace every "I can't" with an "I can."*

—KAYLAN PICKFORD

"I have a confession to make. For most of my driving career, I have not been particularly considerate of other drivers. I tend to drive as if the road were my own private freeway. This began to bother me a few years ago, since it didn't sit too well with the untold hours I have spent as the spokesperson for the Random Acts of Kindness Foundation. I made the commitment to become considerate of others on the road, and then spent a good year disappointing myself over and over again.

"I'd do really well for a while and then suddenly there I was roaring by, blocking some poor soul who was desperately trying to change lanes to get to an exit. I consoled myself that at least I was noticing and regretting my failures. Then at some point it simply stopped being hard at all. It was so gradual I don't even remember how or when, but it became such a normal part of driving habit that in the summer of 1998 I found myself being amazed at the faces of the drivers in Milan (a city internationally known for its aggressive drivers) when I would allow them to cut in.

"When I think about this, it strikes me as a simple but good example of the trajectory of any new behavior we try to. A master at first it is very hard to keep on track, we falter and fail (but at least begin to notice), and then gradually, with discipline and practice, the new behavior begins to take hold until it simply becomes our nature. Learning to live kindly and compassionately in ever-widening circles of community requires just this kind of retraining, but eventually it will simply become who we are."

Today, pick one unkind behavior that you wish to change—interrupting others, for example, or not doing your share of the chores. It has to be something you really *want* to work on. Then make a commitment to practice the behavior you desire for one month. Maybe, like this man, the best you'll do is notice when you fail. That's OK. That's the first step in change. ❧

# Sharing What You Love

*The power of love and caring can
change the world.*

—*James Autry*

A woman in New Orleans who fell in love with the theater in college put her considerable talents to good use creating and promoting an annual celebration of theater that culminates in three straight days of nonstop performances going on simultaneously all over the city.

There is a man in Newark who loves to garden and has a double-sized lot with plenty of space for him to engage his passion. Every year during the summer, a steady stream of locals make their annual pilgrimage past his house. All year long, after work and on weekends, he works in his huge garden, planting and replanting, weeding and trimming, and every year thousands of people drive slowly by to appreciate the fruits of his labor of love.

In the San Francisco area, a collection of people who love to hike not only searched out ways to hike completely around the Bay, but helped set in motion a master plan that will conclude in a few years with a series of publicly maintained hiking trails that circles the Bay.

Each of these people simply followed their passion and shared it with as many people as possible—a fantastic recipe for vibrant community! We all know that we become more animated, more alive, more excited when doing something we love, and the very act of sharing that process with others multiplies that excitement exponentially.

What lights you up, gets your juices flowing? How can you share that with others? True community is created when like-minded people come together over something they love. ❧

# Giving Your Gift

*There is a force, a quickness that is*
*translated through you into action. If you*
*block it, the world will not have it....*

—*MARTHA GRAHAM*

"A few years ago, for my mother's seventieth birthday, we asked everyone in the family, from kids to grandkids, to write stories or poems or draw pictures which were then printed up and bound into a book we presented to her. The day of the party one of the grandchildren announced that she wasn't very good at writing or drawing and that her real talent was her collection of friends, one of whom was at the party. So her contribution was that this particular friend would sing. He stood up and launched into a beautiful rendition of 'Amazing Grace,' which was the high point of the party."

Each of us comes into this life with our own special gift, whether it is a musical ability, a beautiful voice, a talent for sports, a fantastic memory, a great sense of humor, a contagious smile, a laugh that can jump-start a room, a gift for storytelling, or simply a pure zest for life. When we share our gift with others, it creates a powerful resonance that binds us together in the moment of its giving.

For many years the commercial aspects of our world have narrowed the field of gifts considered "of value" to youth and beauty; both have their place, but both have suffered by being elevated to a level they cannot support, and both leave the vast majority of the population believing they are worthless. Our human capacity to amaze and inspire has been relegated to a status of unimportance. What is tragic about this development is not that it can succeed—because ultimately it is the true gifts that surprise and move us—but that it can do so much damage, particularly to the self-confidence of our young as they try to spread their wings and discover the gifts they have to offer.

Whatever special gift you have been given, celebrate it and share as often as possible, and always look out for those special characteristics in others, particularly the young, who need praise and encouragement. ❦

# Do It with Humor

*Laugh and the world laughs with you.*
*Cry and you cry alone.*

—PROVERB

"In college, I read about the victory gardens people planted during the Second World War, and I couldn't understand why they didn't exist any more. So after I was working, I investigated starting a community garden for people who wanted to grow their own vegetables and just hang around with like-minded souls. Little did I know what a bureaucratic maze I would have to go through. 'No, that isn't an appropriate use of city land,' 'Too many liability issues,' 'No way to make sure people won't grow marijuana on city land,' 'Who'd pay for the water?' 'There are serious constitutional issues involved here.' I heard so many fascinating and conflicting excuses for why you couldn't grow vegetables on a piece of city property that no one had done anything with for thirty years, I decided to make a game out of how many excuses they could make up, and at meetings, would relate the list in a humorous way.

"Interestingly, that is precisely what made the garden finally happen. One of the council members finally got as fed up as me with my often-repeated litany of silly excuses and pushed the whole thing through on a trial basis. That trial garden has existed without interruption for eight years now, and we have a steady flow of people coming through, some just curious, some regulars who are serious gardeners, and some who come and go as it suits their schedules. It's a great place to unwind, meet old friends, get your hands dirty, and get some nutritious food for an enjoyable effort."

Sometimes you need a good sense of humor (along with a lot of persistence) to get to where you are headed. Whatever you do, don't let the silliness of bureaucratic excuses get you down or put you off the track. Anger, while it might be righteous, just turns people against you. But humor often wins the day—either all the excuses will run dry, or people will begin to laugh at them, but eventually things of quality always surface over the flotsam and jetsam of life. ❧

# Ask the Meaningful Question

*If love is the answer, could you please
rephrase the question?*

—LILY TOMLIN

"My best friend is the greatest connector to
other people that I have ever known. No matter where she goes, for whatever length of
time—a weekend retreat, a minute long
phone call, a dinner out—she leaves with a
new best friend, a place to stay the next time
she's in Maui, a free upgrade on a flight, a
*gratis* dessert, a deal on a new computer. She
doesn't set out to get these goodies, but she is
naturally warm and real in her interaction,
and that's so rare that other people are overwhelmed with a desire to help her.

"I've watched her closely and found that
the secret is that she asks open-ended questions and genuinely wants to hear the answers:
What are you excited about? What do you like
about your job? What are you looking forward
to? What is difficult for you? What new perspective have you had in the past week? It's
amazing to see what happens to total strangers

when she asks such things. Most people are eager to answer, and soon a connection is made. Every time I see her do it, I vow to try it myself. But I get so self-involved that a whole day slips by before I realize that I haven't asked one person one thing."

We are a culture of statement-makers, trained to know the answers. Questions are seen as a sign of weakness, because they indicate we don't know everything. But of course we don't know everything, particularly the heart of another human being. And the more we inquire of those around us, the more we will encounter the depth, complexity, and uniqueness of those with whom we share our lives, and the more we will learn new ways of looking at a situation.

How about asking one meaningful question today and seeing what is different as a consequence? It has to be a real question, coming from your genuine curiosity, not a statement or judgment disguised as a question. (Don't ask, for example, "How could you be so stupid?") Curiosity won't kill the cat; it will make the bonds between us stronger. ❧

# Respect Your Limits

*If you're not talkin' to yourself, you
talkin' to the wrong people.*

—Cajun proverb

"Recently I worked with a group of people on a local environmental issue. I showed up at my first meeting on the same day as a woman named Joyce, so we were a new-kids-on-the-block team. We were trying to stop the county from developing an area that was a unique habitat and would not survive any kind of development. The whole battle lasted for nearly three years, and in that time I watched Joyce go through at least five cycles of hyper-activity followed by a crash, after which she would be useless for weeks, and then she would start the whole process again.

"I tried to talk to her since it was self-destructive, not to mention very unpleasant to be around, but she couldn't hear it. When she was feeling OK, nothing was as important as the work we were doing and she would throw herself into it completely, staying late, working weekends, ignoring her personal life, and getting into fights with me since my unwillingness to work the same schedule was thrown in my face as lack of commitment. Even after the pattern kept repeating itself, she didn't get it. We ended up delaying the development long enough so that the state stepped in and created a preserve, and I haven't seen Joyce since, but I hope she has figured out how to take better care of herself."

If we are going to make the world a better place, we are going to need all the help we can get. But it doesn't help if we so ignore our own lives that we regularly break down or get furious with those we are working with for their "lack of commitment." We all need rest, recreation, contemplation, and just plain vegging out. It's hard to believe that you can actually accomplish more if you take time for yourself, but it's true.

We love the story Scott Peck tells: "I have a very full and busy life and occasionally I am asked, 'Scotty, how can you do all that you do?' The most telling reply I can give is, 'Because I spend at least two hours a day doing nothing.' Ironically the questioner usually responds by saying he's too busy to do that."

Have you been pushing yourself past your limits? It's not good for you or those around you. Take some time for yourself and notice the difference in how you feel. ❧

# Love the Ones You're With

*There are never enough "I love you"s.*

—LENNY BRUCE

"Why is it you can be the nicest person in the world, always considerate and empathetic with every stranger you meet, and yet be the most inconsiderate, uncompromising jerk around the people you love the most? I have a reputation for being a really sweet person, but I just got a very large lesson in kindness from a small boy. My husband and I had been going back and forth for weeks about a visit to my parents. My husband was trying to wheedle out of about four days of the trip, and I was having none of it.

"We started off on a decent level, politely discussing the different options, but he really wanted out because my parents aren't very nice to him and he is pretty fed up with dealing with it. I wanted him around because when he's there it's a lot easier for me (partly because they direct their irritation toward him, not me). But of course, we weren't talking about the real issues, we were talking about what would be convenient, a good friend he really should visit while he was in the area, some work he should try to get done, and I was taking it all as a reflection of his commitment to me.

"In the midst of all this, we are walking down the mall, and he made some comment about me getting as bad as my mother. I snapped. I don't even remember what I said, but it wasn't nice. The next thing I know this small boy is standing in front of me, saying, 'You shouldn't say things like that.' It would have been funny if it wasn't so embarrassingly true. We expose so much of ourselves to those who are closest to us that we get scared and then, out of fear that we might be hurt, we strike out. It's pretty dumb, because if anyone deserves our compassion and kindness it's the person who is willing to put up with all of our idiosyncrasies. I thanked that little boy for the reminder, and my husband and I worked out a compromise that met both of our needs."

Why *is* it easier sometimes to be kind to even the most unlovable stranger than to those with whom we share our homes and lives? Whatever the reasons, if we want to live in a world full of love, we need to be sure to spread some around close to home as well as across the sea. 🖤

## Don't Give Up

*Trust in what you love, continue to do it, and it will take you where you need to go.*

—NATALIE GOLDBERG

There is a woman who is a minor legend among the insiders at city hall in Los Angeles. She is very quiet and polite, and she showed up for virtually every single council meeting for over thirty years to speak up for a more aggressive budget for the Parks and Recreation Department. At first people were amused. Here this quiet little lady would get up and, in the middle of an agenda full of heated issues and grand controversy, would ask that some money be allocated for a swimming pool in South Central to give the kids something constructive to do on a hot summer day. Gradually they got irritated. Instead of a nice polite lady she seemed more and more like a buzzing mosquito that wouldn't go away. Eventually she became so much a part of the proceeding that everyone knew her by name and treated her like an old friend, even if they were ignoring her requests for a new park here or some repairs there, or new playground equipment for some aging park area.

Over the years, very gradually and almost unnoticeably, she began to get some of the things she asked for. It was almost as though, because she had become a good friend of everyone involved, they could only refuse her so many times and were embarrassed not to give in now and then. It helped that her requests were always reasonable, always relatively modest (especially in light of the huge budgets of the City of Los Angeles) and always backed up with very sound research and documentation. And it helped that she never attacked, never accused the council of bad faith or wrong-headed priorities (even though she often had cause).

Eventually she became one of the most

effective lobbyists in the city. Even during times when budgets were being slashed across the board, the Parks and Rec Department continued a modest but significant growth. Simply by persisting, by always being there, by demonstrating her good will and sincere intent over and over again, she became an almost irresistible force. It is a lesson we can all profit from. ✎

## Come from the Heart

*Surely the earth can be saved by all the*
*people who insist on love.*
—ALICE WALKER

"When I was in college, I was in an anti-Vietnam War group with a guy who was incredibly smart and had a real talent for seeing what was going on and summing it all up in ways that were easy to understand. His one problem was that he would get completely frustrated when people didn't understand his point. He married a woman who had a reputation for being somewhat flighty (as in not terribly interested in all-night meetings and long intellectual arguments).

"Over the years I kept in touch with them, visiting every few years. Neither of them changed dramatically, but gradually I began to see them in a different light. His clarity of vision stayed with him, but combined with his frustration over people's inability to 'understand,' he was slowly becoming more difficult to work with, more impatient, and slightly bitter, as if he expected people to get it, whatever 'it' was, wrong. On the other hand, she just blossomed. People are drawn to her, because it is so apparent that she is real and grounded in a true appreciation and concern for everything and everyone around her.

"On one visit, I got to witness the two of them in action at a local meeting about a proposal to build low-income housing in the neighborhood. They lived in a nice middle-class area and this was a hotly debated issue. He did a fantastic job of laying out the facts, but it was clear that it wasn't working. Then his wife started quietly working the room, and by time the meeting was over the project had been approved.

"What struck me was that as good as my friend was in his head, it was his wife who was most effective because she was authentic. She came from the heart and people could feel that her beliefs were a living, breathing part of herself and not simply an intellectual exercise. Trying to build community requires our whole self in order to work. What brings people together, truly, is the feelings that are created between them, much more than the intellectual understanding that something is the right thing to do. We need to learn to live what we desire, because in that way we become magnets to draw people along."

# 9

# Giving from Plenty

The only certain measure of success
is to render more and better service
than is expected of you.

—OG MANDINO

In the process of building community, whether the community is a stronger family, a wider network of friends, a neighborhood association, or an international movement, the most significant breakthrough comes when we learn how to give from plenty.

For most of our lives, whether consciously or not, we have operated on a classic two-column ledger system—what is given in one column must be taken away from the other. It is a formula with winners and losers, getters and givers, perpetrators and victims, donors and supplicants. The rules of barter, negotiation, and exchange so permeate our society and relationships that it can be hard even to conceive of a different way. We are constantly hoarding our assets—both time and money—and doling them out carefully and reluctantly.

But there is a different way, one that doesn't require winners and losers and doesn't distort our intentions or relationships. It is the realization that the more we give, the richer we become. Most of us find our way there accidentally. We stumble on someone in need and do whatever is called for without question, only to discover that we have been enriched by the act of giving.

Without this perspective, when most of us look at our lives all we see are the things we don't have instead of how incredibly blessed we are. The truth is we are the richest and most privileged generation ever to inhabit the Earth. We have medical technology that grants us a life-span three times that of our ancestors; we have economic and social stability that have never been seen before; we have so many options that our biggest problem has become choosing, when for most of history people had no choices at all. We are overflowing with things: things to play with, things to make our work easier and more productive, extraordinarily beautiful things, which historically would have been the property only of kings and queens, to hang on our walls. We can call forth the world's most beautiful music at a moment's notice; we can visit the wonders of the world at our leisure in person or via computer.

We are swimming in a world of plenty, and yet all we see are the holes. It is high time we took off the blinders. Each one of us has riches and resources beyond the imagination of 99 percent of the people who previously inhabited this planet. When we live from a feeling of plenty, we will find plenty of places to spend ourselves freely.

# Loving from Overflow

*Real charity doesn't care if it's
deductible or not.*

—*ANONYMOUS*

"My father was a small-town family doctor, the old-fashioned kind who made house calls, birthed babies, and comforted the dying when they were beyond medical care. Everyone in town knew him and assumed that we were rich, because he was a doctor. But my father, who had grown up in the slums of Boston, was never rich, because he kept his fees low and gave away a lot of care for free. It used to drive my mother crazy, because she always wanted to stockpile money for 'the future.'

"This was in the days before medical insurance and all the talk was about the coming of socialized medicine. He didn't believe in it, he said, because he thought every doctor should volunteer to see a percentage of patients for free. If every doctor did, then everyone would have adequate medical care. When he retired, I helped him close down his office. I was

271

supposed to send out final bills, but mostly I just listened to him tell me why so and so could not pay and so should not be charged. He knew everyone's story.

"When I asked him why he wasn't more concerned about money, he said that given his background, he felt very rich and didn't need any more than he already had, and that it was his honor to be able to give his medical gift to as many people as possible. We may never have been affluent, but when he died this year, twenty years after retirement, the church was packed with former patients, nurses, and doctors who came to say thanks to a man with a big heart. Because he felt rich, he was."

So many of us think that safety lies in accumulating a big wad of money. But stock markets can crash and banks can fail. Our true safety lies in creating a strong network of loving family, friends, and neighbors, who will be there for us, no matter what happens. ❧

# Greater and Greater Communion

*Always be open-handed with your brother,*
*and with anyone in your country*
*who is in need.*

—DEUTERONOMY

"I used to get irritated at the homeless people who hung around the office building where I worked. They made me feel guilty and angry at the same time, and so I never stopped to give anyone money. Then, three years after moving here to take a job, I was fired. Actually, I drank myself out of a job. A few months later, there I was, on the street myself.

"I was homeless for almost a year before I was able to clean myself up and find a new job, but I wouldn't have made it at all if it weren't for a lot of people who helped me along the way. When I hit bottom, I discovered what generosity really meant. One of my first nights on the street I was befriended by a couple of guys who shared their food with me and filled me in on all the details I needed to know: where the shelters were if it got too cold; which places you had to be careful about; good spots to sleep in relative safety; places you could get or find food, and what time you had to be there. They also warned me about drinking in the wrong places. A lot of the tolerance for homeless people depended on how offensive you were, and in the wrong condition I could be pretty offensive. By the time I had straightened my life out, more than a dozen people, most of them in as much trouble as I was, had given me a helping hand somewhere along the line."

It's so easy to go into a scarcity mentality in which all our energy goes into getting things for ourselves. We begin to believe there isn't enough of anything, so we better make sure we've got ours—then maybe we can afford to give to others. But when is enough enough? A recent study showed that no matter how much money people made, they believed they would be happy if they had more. It didn't matter if they earned $20,000 or $200,000—everyone felt they needed just a bit more. Obviously, from the scarcity perspective, there never will be enough.

Ironically, living with that attitude, which

we believe will keep us safe, actually impoverishes us by pulling us further and further away from others. Conversely, when we operate from an attitude of plenty, when we assume that the more we give the more we will receive, we are drawn together into greater and greater communion with others. ❧

## Stop Caring about Blame and Credit

*Be the change you want to see in the world.*

—*GANDHI*

"I worked on a very intensive two-year research project with a consultant we jokingly called 'Saint Nick.' The time pressure was deadly, the area we were in was very complex, and it was easy to make small mistakes that could take you way out of your territory. We had a team of thirty-four highly educated, high-ego individuals trying to act cooperatively. When one part of the team fell behind or made mistakes that impacted another part, teeth would start grinding and curt comments would follow, and if it weren't for Nick, it would have escalated quickly into all-out attack/defense mode.

"In retrospect, there was nothing particularly fancy about how he handled people. But he never got upset, he never accused or blamed, and he always seemed to enjoy himself, as though everything that happened was a part of some fascinating adventure. When people got hot under the collar, he'd smile and smooth things over. When people started attacking and defending, he'd very calmly turn the discussion into a constructive analysis of what could be done to get back on track. Even when someone very clearly made a mistake that had cost time and effort, he would take it completely in stride and derail the finger-pointers.

"At the successful completion of the project, Nick complimented us, said we were a fantastic group to work with, and that he'd had a lot of fun. I really think he did too, even though it is hard to imagine how baby-sitting a large group of spoiled scientists could be fun. I do know that I learned more about how to be a decent person in those two years than in the previous thirty-eight years of my life."

When we simply stop trying to assign blame and apportion credit, life becomes so much simpler and so much more enjoyable. We have such a strong individualist streak in our culture that we tend to reduce everything to what I did right and what you did wrong, but a community doesn't operate that way. Regardless of the different contributions from its members, a community is always a collective effort. ❦

## Remembering What Matters

*Deep within man dwells slumbering powers; powers that would astonish him, that he never dreamed of possessing; forces that would revolutionize his life if aroused and put into action.*

—ORISON SWETT MARDEN

"I lived for a few years next door to man who literally hoarded everything that ever passed through his hands. It was a very sad situation (not to mention a significant health hazard), since his entire house, yard, and drive-way was stacked to shoulder height with things. The city was in a constant battle with him to clean up the mess, and he'd always agree and then just move one pile from one place to another, and the process would start all over.

"One day his daughter came by to apologize to me for the inconvenience of his hoarding. She was very nice and very embarrassed. She wanted to reassure me that her father wasn't dangerous or crazy, and in trying to explain her father's behavior, she ended up saying he had a 'scarcity mentality,' which I though was a very polite way to put it. It really summed it up very neatly. Her father was afraid that there wouldn't be enough of anything and from that perspective, I could see how it would be terribly wrong to throw anything away. The irony was that my neighbor had too much stuff to ever find anything if he ever needed to, much less use it.

"The more I thought about it, the more I wondered why this man's extreme behavior wasn't more common, since our culture very aggressively promotes exactly the fear that none of us has enough: enough toys, cars, appliances, clothes, shoes, CDs, you name it. We are bombarded daily by advertisements insisting we need more stuff, and by the cultural deification of the rich and famous, who have all this stuff. The worth of an individual gets reduced to the quantity and quality of our stuff, and our time gets taken by acquiring and then caring for all our stuff."

In fact, long before we get our first credit card, we all possess a wealth of the most valuable resource there is—love and compassion. And the most amazing thing about this personal treasure is that the more you give away the richer you become.

Take a moment to think about your relationship to the "stuff" in your life. Do you spend as much time connecting to those you love as you do purchasing, cleaning, and maintaining your stuff? ❧

# Becoming Expansive

*When we quit thinking primarily about
ourselves and our self-preservation, we
undergo a truly heroic transformation
of consciousness.*

—JOSEPH CAMPBELL

"I visited a classroom of third-graders once to talk about kindness, and in the excited interchange I asked them why they thought people should be kind to each other. I got a lot of the usual answers: Because it's nice, because it makes people feel good, because then they'll be nice to you. Then one girl said, 'Because when you're nice and share with people it makes you big, and when you're mean and won't share with people it makes you smaller.' To this day, I think that is one of the best answers I've ever heard."

Practicing kindness is expansive. It makes us grow, it extends our influence further and further out into the world, and connects us in very powerful ways with the lives of those we touch, and that in return is powerfully invigorating.

Conversely, when we withhold our compassion from the world, when we pull back and retreat into our private fortress and hoard our assets, we shrink into a smaller and smaller space, outside the pulsing flow of life all around us. Cut off from the most fundamental human exchange, we have less and less access to our hearts.

The irony of course is that the consequences of our decisions impact our own lives with considerable more force than they affect others. When we refuse to extend a helping hand, an opportunity for assistance or empathy may be lost to others, but it is our own life that is most harmed. For in cutting ourselves off, we are also severing our connection to the very things that can make life so joyful. When do reach out, no matter how tired or busy we might be, we become larger, more full of love and tenderness, more able to be moved by life, more complete. ❧

# Teach Your Children Well

*No one has yet fully realized the wealth
of sympathy, kindness, and generosity
hidden in the soul of the child.*

—*EMMA GOLDMAN*

"A friend of mine is a successful self-made businessman. He remembers well the snotty spoiled rich kids in his school, and he worries all the time that his success, and particularly his money, will spoil his children and make them insensitive to others. He needn't worry; he has done a great job of raising them. They are great kids, I believe, because he's put a lot of effort into teaching them to be kind and generous. Twenty-five percent of their weekly allowance gets put instantly into a separate box to be given away as each child determines. Sometimes they 'borrow' from their mom or dad to give money to a homeless person and then pay it out of their box when they get home; sometimes they plan to save it up and buy toys for less privileged kids at Christmas; and sometimes they send some money in response to a news story. Because it is their money and their responsibility, they actually talk about where they should give their money to do the most good. This is not the typical middle-class America dinner-time conversation!

"Another tradition he has instituted is monthly assistance at a local church soup kitchen. The whole family shows up one Saturday a month and sets tables, scrubs pots and pans, chops vegetables, and does anything else needed in the serving and cleanup of a meal for 300 people. While the kids often complain, mainly when it interferes with either their baseball or soccer season, once they get there they work hard and seem to enjoy it. And they are always telling stories about the people who come in and the jokes they tell—as you can imagine, the kids are the hit of kitchen and are doted upon not only by the kitchen staff, but by most of the clientele as well."

These kids are incredibly lucky, because they have been introduced at a very early age to the plentiful grace of giving. The experience of making a strong positive impact on other peoples' lives at such a young age is a priceless gift, one we should all bestow on our children. Reflect for a moment on what you can do to help the kids in your sphere of influence become more kind and caring citizens of the Earth. ❧

# The Joy of Service

*Small service is true service.... The daisy, by
the shadow that it casts, protects the
lingering dewdrop from the sun.*

—WILLIAM WORDSWORTH

"One evening I was on a call-in radio show
about kindness, and I got a call from a man in
New York who worked on Wall Street as a
stock analyst. He told me that even though it
might sound funny to some people, he loved
his work. It was challenging and besides pro-
viding him with a very good living for his
family, it gave him the satisfaction of doing
something really well.

"That wasn't what he'd called to talk about
though. Since his work was all about numbers and trends and money, it didn't satisfy
his need to feel like he was doing something
of value in the world. His way of dealing
with that need was to volunteer at a homeless
shelter. After a few months of quietly doing
whatever was requested of him, his analyst
mind started to click in and he figured at
least some of these homeless people would

be able to get jobs but most of them were not terribly presentable and would undoubtedly not make much of an impression at an interview. He started offering a laundry service to people looking for jobs. He'd pick up the clothes on Friday, do the laundry at home on the weekend, and bring it in Monday morning on his way to work. Then he began to stock a small closet at the shelter with shirts, pants, ties, suits, and sport coats that came from his closet and those of a handful of friends who were willing to help out.

"But that wasn't what he called to talk about either. What he wanted to say was that the opportunity to work with these homeless men was the thing that kept him sane and happy. It was the one place in his life where he really felt like he was making a difference that mattered."

It is a mark of a person's depth when they realize that what they can offer to others is what's most important in life. The small step from feeling obligated to perform service to appreciating the opportunity to do it is the mark of true awareness, and the opportunity for true joy. If you've been thinking you "should" do something for others, pick something you might truly enjoy—and then see how much joy it brings. ❧

## Making Time

*When God made time, he made plenty of it.*
—*IRISH PROVERB*

Most of us would love to be a part of something bigger than ourselves, whether it is helping those in need or participating in connections to others, but there just doesn't seem to be enough time. There is so much to do to take care of ourselves and our family and so little time to do it in. The "American dream" seems to involve working long hours, commuting over long distances, squeezing out a little socializing, and spending the rest of the time slumped in front of the television recuperating, so we can get up and start all over again the next day.

Most of us do not have the luxury of a job that allows us to make a living at our passion and at the same time provides us the opportunity to offer our unique talents to the service of others. Instead of a society structured to support and encourage such a combination, it seems as though society was designed to make it as difficult as possible. Our society sends a very clear message on how we value such professions, since most of them—teachers, ministers, social workers, legal aid and medical clinic workers—are at the bottom of the pay scale. And what if our talents run in different directions? It's not so easy for a mathematician to combine job and service. Most of us have to find the time in our "spare" hours.

Pressure from women and a growing number of men concerned about having time to spend with their children has already begun to slow down the treadmill we're on. We need to introduce into our workplaces the concept that we all have many priorities in our lives and need the time to pursue them. Does your company have a policy that allows you to do community service during work time? (Many now do.) Perhaps you can initiate the conversation that might result in such a policy.

We need to be creative and flexible when finding time for doing service. Despite how busy we are, most of us truly do have time to spare. Maybe an hour a week driving meals to AIDS patients works best; maybe being a Big Sister one Saturday morning a month fits your schedule better. Only you know what will work for you. ❧

## Take Time for Yourself

*Aloneness and connection are like tides*
*in the sea of your heart,*
*separate tides flowing in and out.*
—*M. C. Richards*

"My work as a stockbroker has dictated the pace of my life. Usually I have no regrets. The fast pace, the excitement and gamble, never knowing what will reveal itself around the next bend, makes me feel like a modern-day explorer. The ten- to twelve-hour days don't leave me much time but, ironically, I've discovered that if I take one half-hour to be completely quiet and alone, I am then more available for my husband, kids, friends, and neighbors than if I rush home right away.

"Our condo is about a half-hour walk from Wall Street, and in good weather I walk home. Being in the air, with no one pulling on me for anything, clears out everything from the frenetic Wall Street energy to the cobwebs of exhaustion. I head home, fresher and more open, ready to respond to whoever might need me."

In the hustle and bustle of our days, it's easy to feel that we can't possibly manage any time for ourselves. Yet one of the best things we can do to improve our ability to respond to other people is to take time alone. Perhaps one of the reasons so many of us are unwilling or unable to extend ourselves to those around us is that we spend so little time alone, in quiet contemplation. We are not limitless givers; we need to come back to our core and replenish ourselves, or we will have nothing to give. As M. C. Richards alludes, if the tide only went out, soon there would be no water left at all.

Only you know what replenishes you—a walk in nature, a swim at the gym, fifteen minutes of meditation, a hot bath. When we give to ourselves, we make it more possible to give generously to others. ❧

# 10

# We Are a Community of Kindness

Only those who risk going
too far can possibly find out
how far one can go.

—*T. S. Eliot*

*Some people say that a new era* in human history began when the first photos of our world were beamed back to Earth from outer space, and for the first time we could see planet Earth, extraordinarily beautiful in its vibrant colors, yet hanging isolated in a massive unending sea of black universe. From the outside, we saw the truth of what we are—one robust but fragile community, inextricably bound together, and unalterably responsible for the future of ourselves and our planet.

To consciously exercise that responsibility, we need to put aside our comfortable but narrow perspectives and become masters at seeing the multidimensional world we live in. We exist in a beautifully complex set of nested communities, each of which connects us by an amazing array of threads to everything and everyone else in the world. We exist as individuals, bound into family units, tied closely with circles of friends and acquaintances, encompassed in our local and chosen communities, contained within increasingly large communities defined by language, race, religion, and geography, all embedded within the larger community of the Earth itself.

And the connective tissue that holds this amazingly intricate set of connections together is our greatest treasure, our capacity for kindness and compassion. Our work is to apply this powerful resource to our new perspective of interconnectedness to bind us closer and more joyfully together.

## Six Degrees of Separation

*If you are unfaithfully here, you are causing
great damage. But if your love is joined to the
great Love, you are helping people you don't
know and have never met.*

—*Rumi*

Every one of us has probably noticed that
we can strike up a conversation with a total
stranger, and if we delve deep enough, there
is bound to be a person we have in common—I know a man whose sister's best
friend rented a house from your aunt; my
second cousin's wife went to college with
your best friend. This has been characterized
as "six degrees of separation," meaning you
will never have to go through a chain of more
than six people to find a connection to anyone else in the world. It's always fun to try to
track down the connections, and at the same
time it's almost unbelievable how often you
actually find a common link.

Now it appears not so surprising at all.
Mathematicians at Cornell and Columbia uni-
versities have developed a model that explains

how and why it is such a small world after all. The key is what used to be the relatively small number of people who traveled to many places and knew lots of people. They created a hub of connections, which then jumped randomly around the world, thereby connecting more and more people to each other much more rapidly.

Today, with all the traveling that people have done over the last thirty years, the number of "hub" people has multiplied so much that we truly are a small world. And the potential consequences are huge. On the one hand, this phenomenon fueled the AIDS crisis (a few years ago, scientists traced the epidemic back to one source, an airline employee who was at the center of such a hub) and the spread of other diseases. But it also means that kindness and peace and new thinking about how to relate better to each other can also spread like wildfire.

What that means, truly, is that the actions we take on a daily basis ripple out into the world and affect the lives of people we will never meet. Let us build on the closeness of those connections and help turn our small world into one where people not only are connected but build mutually supportive bridges to one another. ∿

## No Action Too Small

*You cannot do a kindness too soon, because you never know how soon it will be too late.*

—RALPH WALDO EMERSON

"I read a story recently about a poor working-class man in the early part of the twentieth century who went on to become a major political force in England because of the unintentional kindness of a young girl. He was kept sitting in a manor house for a long time, waiting to speak to the lady of the house, who deemed him not important enough for her to appear on time. He was fuming with class hatred when suddenly a very small girl holding a book opened the door to the parlor. Her appearance only fueled his rage further—here was this beautiful little girl in a fancy dress all full of herself when his own sister was starving in a cottage down the hill.

"Coming across the room, the little girl handed him the book, and looking at him with a gaze of loving trust, said, 'Please will you read to me?' In that moment, tears sprung to his eyes and all anger fled, as the innocence of the child opened his heart. He happily complied, and when the mistress of the house appeared about ten minutes later, it was to meet a man in a vastly different mood than only a few moments before. The woman was so taken with him that she became his political patron, and he ultimately rose to national prominence and was able to greatly help the poor people of his district. 'I might say that to the chance entry of that child,' he wrote, 'I owe all the achievement in the world for which, rightly or wrongly, I have received honor.'"

Every day, we have hundreds of opportunities to influence our world and the people in it. Like the little girl in this story, we may even alter the course of history by the simplest of acts. ❧

# Seeing Deeply the Interconnections

*Each element of the cosmos is positively woven from all of the others. . . . The universe holds together, and only one way of considering it is really possible, that is, to take it as a whole, in one piece.*

—*Teilhard de Chardin*

"I remember a few years back when the U.S. economy wasn't doing terribly well and a coalition of organizations put together a 'Buy America' campaign to convince people to buy American-made products. It garnered a little news coverage, and they got out a lot of bumper stickers, but overall it didn't have much of an impact on what people were buying, since in general consumers try to get the best product for the least amount of money. A little while later I read an article with a detailed list of where different parts on an 'American-made' car were manufactured—it covered a good portion of the globe!"

To anyone who looks beyond the surface, the threads of international connection in our lives are everywhere. From the peasants of Peru who picked the beans for our morning coffee to the machinist in Korea who ground the gears on our car's transmission, to the Mexican tomato farmer who helped supply our dinner salad, we cannot go through a day without relying upon the labor and skills of thousands of people around the world.

We may not all identify ourselves as citizens of the world, but in our material world, this has been true for some time. We need now to act on that realization by treating each part of our community, from the coffee plantation workers in South America to the factory workers in Asia to the software developers in California, with respect and kindness, and planning for a future that considers the needs of us all.

One way to make that real is to take time to contemplate the origins of the food on your plate at dinner. A Zen Buddhist blessing says, "Innumerable labors brought us this food; we should know how it comes to us." Can you see the sunshine, the rain, the farmworkers, the truckers, grocery clerks, the person who cooked it? We're all part of a vast chain. 🐦

# Our Neighbors across the Globe

*Our actions may be impure and set
up a stream of reactions, but always we
can come again to the seed of pure mind and
right relationship. . . . The common kernel is
care for all beings, good relationship,
cycles of reciprocity, generosity. . . .*
—DHYANI YWAHOO

"My grandfather was an old union organizer who got equally upset about the state of labor unions today and what he perceived as the strong anti-union sentiment in this country. The whole point, he used to say, was that everyone deserved decent wages and safe working conditions, and that, more than anything else, was what the labor movement was all about. Then he would launch into stories about how hard they had to work to get people in the same town, people who were neighbors of the workers, to understand and appreciate the importance of what the workers were doing.

"One of the things that made him really happy was to watch the success of the United

Farm Workers. He thought it was just great that they had mounted a national campaign convincing people to forgo eating grapes or lettuce for the sake of decent wages and safe working conditions. To him, that was a real sign that people were becoming more aware and more concerned about other people's lives.

"My grandfather died a few years ago, but I know he would be tickled pink over the recent flurry of activity surrounding sweatshop conditions and low wages paid by American companies to workers all across Asia. That's always been business as usual, now you have the president of Nike running scared, the heads of major fashion apparel companies scrambling to force their subcontractors to clean up working conditions, and a growing movement within the United States, led by an organization called Businesses for Social Responsibility, to require that working conditions and wage levels in developing countries be monitored so that the horrendous exploitation that has characterized that unequal relationship can be eliminated.

"My grandfather would have thought it a pretty good sign for the survival of humanity that we can sit in our comfortable homes and still express concern for decent conditions and wages across the world with enough force to alter corporate behavior."

We vote with our dollars as well as at the ballot box. Where we choose to spend our money gives tacit support to the business practices of the companies we patronize. As we create a community of kindness, we will want to support those companies whose values are in alignment with our own—and pressure other companies into socially responsible actions. Do you feel good about the companies you buy from? The places you invest your money? ❧

# Opening Our Hearts

*We are one world ... and one great human problem and what we do here goes to solve not only our petty troubles alone but the difficulties and desires of millions unborn and unknown. Let us then realize our responsibilities and gain strength to bear them worthily.*

—W. E. B. Du Bois

In any time of social change there are issues and events that seem specially designed to test our resolve, to stretch to the absolute maximum our capacity for compassion and our commitment to an inclusive definition of community. AIDS is one such issue.

While new combinations of drugs have created optimism in much of the developed world, the real tragedy and the ultimate challenge lies in the developing parts of the world, particularly in Africa. According to recent figures, AIDS now infects 25 percent of the adults in Botswana and Zimbabwe, and at least 10 percent of the adults in eleven other African countries. Already 30 million people, the vast majority of them living in Africa, are infected, and that number is expected to rise to 40 million by the year 2000. Barring a miracle, most of those infected are fated to die, since they live in countries too impoverished and too poorly run to provide adequate health care.

By contrast, the two greatest previous epidemics in history—the Black Plague, which swept Europe in the Middle Ages, and the worldwide influenza epidemic in 1918 and 1919—left 20 million people dead in their wake. We are poised then not only to witness, but to be a party to, the greatest epidemic in recorded history. It is no secret that the continent of Africa, birthplace of our species, has been treated as a disposable commodity in this past century. Awash in poverty and torn apart by internal struggles rooted in the most brutal kinds of tribalism, Africa is not a place we want to think about. Until now, the developed world's sole contributions have been sporadic famine relief and advanced weaponry. But if we are to emerge as a people committed to compassion and community in the broadest sense of those terms, then we must begin again in Africa.

Each of us must look into our own heart and find a way to stay awake to the problem, so that we can respond in a compassionate way. None of us has the answers, but that doesn't mean we should go numb to the questions such suffering raises. If we can keep our hearts open, we will find ways to be truly helpful. ❧

## Finding Our True Destiny

*Most people see what is,*
*and never see what can be.*

—ALBERT EINSTEIN

As a people, we have always been obsessed with our destiny, our place in the grand sweep of history, and more often than not our response to this issue has been to grow and expand. Kingdoms and empires have risen and fallen to the rhetoric of "divine right," "noblesse oblige," "manifest destiny," and "Lieberstrum!" No matter where we are from, we have wanted to be the biggest, the most powerful, the best: to have the most beautiful cities, the best writers and artists, the biggest and best churches. Be the first at everything, conquer the seas, explore the unexplored, conquer the stars. Our mad rush forward has brought us abruptly up against a barrier that has changed the entire picture: at least temporarily, we have run out of easily accessible places to expand into.

The universe around us is vast. We peer out from our tiny little planet at stars and planets tens if not hundreds of light-years away and know that we have been brought up short. And in the flow of time, perhaps this is not such a bad thing, because we have been given an opportunity to redefine our destiny so that it includes things more fundamental and essential than expansion and competition.

In the meantime, we have squandered many natural resources in our mad rush to get to the edge of our planet, and now we are figuratively standing shoulder to shoulder, packed tightly together. Perhaps this is a none-too-subtle hint that our true destiny is not about conquering things or people or places, but about learning how to live together in harmony. For we have come to a juncture where that is the only viable option left. We cannot continue to fight among ourselves, for we have the means to destroy all life and will undoubtedly eventually do so if we don't end that pursuit. We cannot continue to exploit mindlessly the bounty of Earth, because we are already close to depleting the very resources we will need to survive. And we can no longer be content fighting to be king of the lifestyle mountain, since the press of humanity surrounding us simply and rightly will not stand for such glaring differences.

We are left with no choice if we want to survive. Our challenge, our true destiny, is to turn living together in peace and kindness into an art form. Each one of us has a part to play. What is yours? ❧

## Engaging with Life

*I think we too often make choices based on
the safety of cynicism, and what we're led to
is a life not fully lived. Cynicism is fear,
and worse than fear—it's an active
disengagement. It says, "I don't
have to ask a question."*

—Ken Burns

"When I first got out of college, I worked as a journalist for a few years. During that time, I became close friends with Mark, who was almost as young as I was, but had been writing for newspapers for three years already, and had the hard-core journalist thing down pat—drinking twenty cups of coffee a day, smoking like mad, and being completely cynical about everything.

"I'm embarrassed to say I looked up to Mark, probably because he was so completely unwilling to grant anyone even the possibility of a decent motive, and at the time it not only fit into my young man's wannabe self-image, but it seemed worldly and knowledgeable. Ultimately, I was spared the pitfalls of serious cynicism because I laughed too easily and liked people too quickly, but it captured Mark like a virulent disease. For awhile I thought it was really just an act, or if not an act, at least just a surface distrust that could be gotten through.

"Mark used to blame his distrust on a woman named Lisa, with whom he had fallen in love, and who had broken his heart. I never could get the rest of the story, and in all the years I knew him I was never able to get past all his cynical defenses. When I left the paper, we were not on good terms.

"Years later I ran into the infamous Lisa quite accidentally at a party. We started telling Mark stories (of which there were quite a few) and after a while I asked her what had really happened between them. She started crying and told me he was the love of her life, but after four breakups and reunions, she decided it just wasn't worth it—no matter what, he wouldn't give up his cynicism, and to her it was as if he refused to be a part of the world."

It's so easy to be cynical—we all have plenty of evidence that the world is going to hell in a handbasket, people only are interested in themselves, and no one can be trusted. But, as Ken Burns points out, cynicism is the coward's way out. It allows us to sit in the safety of our assumptions, never taking the risk required to engage fully with life. Yes, we might get hurt if we offer our heart to another; yes, we might fail at creating the kind of community we want; yes, we might not be able to preserve the environment. But *at least we will have tried*. And in the trying, we will find love and laughter, connection and meaning.

If we risk nothing, we will stay small. But if we take the risk of reaching out in kindness and compassion to those near and far, our souls will grow large with the richness that such connections bring, and we will have the deep-in-the-bones sense of satisfaction that comes from using ourselves up for a grand cause. ❧

# A Part of the Whole

*Everything that is done in the world
is done by hope.*

—MARTIN LUTHER KING, JR.

The incredible and spontaneous growth of
the Random Acts of Kindness (RAK) movement took us very much by surprise, so much
so that the RAK Foundation has been running
like mad the last few years just to keep up
with people's demand. It is a fundamental
symbol of the changes that are taking place all
around the world: tens of thousands of people, donating their time and energy to
encourage their neighborhoods, schools,
towns, or states into acting from a place of
greater compassion.

At the RAK Foundation, we were so focused
on getting the community packet out or
responding to questions and suggestions for
activities, we barely noticed when the kindness movement went international. It wasn't
Canada, it was Colleen and Debbie; not
Australia, but Brian. Sure we have Chinese,
Italian, British, German, and Swedish

members, but what does it mean? So it was really a surprise when we received an invitation from the Japanese Small Kindness Movement to come to Tokyo, and we did, first in 1996. There we met up with like-minded people from Japan, Singapore, Thailand, England, Canada, and Australia, and began to explore ways that we might cooperate. In 1997 we returned and founded the International Kindness Movement. In 1998 we began planning for an international kindness event in the year 2000.

So what *does* it all mean? Certainly people's powerful dedication and commitment is partly a reaction to a world that has seen so much hatred and cruelty it has seemingly lost touch with what is important. More than anything, however, it is a genuine and deeply rooted expression of people's desire to start over fresh, to reestablish a moral order, a standard against which all our actions will be measured. This desire—that in all things we treat each other with kindness and compassion—transcends alliance or allegiance, borders and boundaries.

We hope that knowing about this international upswelling gives you hope (it certainly does for us) and the inspiration to find ways to create meaningful connections wherever you live and however they are important to you. Together we *can* make a difference. ❧

# ACKNOWLEDGMENTS

MANY THANKS TO THE THOUSANDS OF PEOPLE all over the country who have written to the Random Acts of Kindness Foundation or to Conari Press, who have sent e-mails to our Web site, and who have called in to the hundreds of radio call-in shows that have hosted Random Acts of Kindness programs. These people's stories, their desires, their memories, and their dreams, form the core of this book.

Thanks in particular to Melissa Fumia of the Random Acts of Kindness Foundation, Emily Miles and Leslie Rossman for their fabulous publicity efforts over the years on behalf of the kindness movement, and authors Dawna Markova and Daphne Rose Kingma for their wise counsel on kindness and community. Thanks also to past and present staff members of Conari Press for their support of the kindness movement (lots of phones answered, orders filled, and materials sent out), for their nurturing of this and all our books, and for the teachings in community they continue to provide. Current staffers are Tom King, Annette Madden, Heather Dever, Everton Lopez, Nancy Margolis, Brenda Knight, Robin Demers, Suzanne Albertson, Claudia Smelser, Sharon Donovan, Nina Lesowitz, Sabirah Mustafa, and Claudia Schaab. Thanks, too, to our families for stories, love, inspiration, and their understanding of the time we spent on this book.

We also acknowledge the communities we are privileged to be current members of, as well as the many we have participated in over the past twenty-five years. The lessons have not all been easy, but they have all been worthwhile.

—*WILL GLENNON AND MARY JANE RYAN, EDITORS OF CONARI PRESS*

## ABOUT THE RANDOM ACTS OF
## KINDNESS FOUNDATION

THE BOOK, RANDOM ACTS OF KINDNESS, was published in February 1993 and sparked great interest throughout the country from newspapers and radio talk shows that began interviewing local kindness crusaders and celebrating their deeds. Overwhelmed by responding readers who wanted to do something to "help spread the kindness movement," Conari Press created the Random Acts of Kindness (RAK) Foundation and announced the first Random Acts of Kindness Week celebration for February 1995.

Coordinated and supported by the Random Acts of Kindness Foundation, participants in the first Random Acts of Kindness Week included over 140 communities coast-to-coast—from Boston to Los Angeles, and from Lubbock to Yukon, as well as thousands of schools, city governments, and nonprofit organizations. Each year since 1995 the Random Acts of Kindness Week celebration has nearly doubled in size, with over 450 communities and thousands of schools and service organizations in the United States, Canada, Australia, Japan, Singapore, Thailand, Italy, and England participating in 1998.

## The Random Acts of Kindness Foundation

The Random Acts of Kindness Foundation is a California 501(c)(3) corporation that acts as a touchstone and support for thousands of people who are committed to spreading kindness throughout the world. The Foundation serves two functions: it provides information on setting up ongoing kindness programs, and organizes the annual RAK Week campaign. This year the Foundation is devoting its time and resources to three new projects. It will be promoting a membership program to better organize and assist its existing community coordinators and RAK enthusiasts. It will be developing a new Web site that is more comprehensive and interactive. And finally it will be expanding its "Kindness in the Schools" program and developing a RAK employee wellness program for businesses and organizations.

## Join the Kindness Crusade!

If you would like to become a member of the Random Acts of Kindness Foundation and/or you would like information about participating in the annual Random Acts of Kindness Week celebration, please contact the RAK Foundation office at 800-660-2811 or e-mail RAKDAY@aol.com.

Conari Press, established in 1987,
publishes books on topics ranging from
psychology, spirituality, and women's history
to sexuality, parenting, and personal growth.
Our main goal is to publish quality books
that will make a difference in people's lives—
both how we feel about ourselves and
how we relate to one another.

Our readers are our most important resource,
and we value your input, suggestions,
and ideas. We'd love to hear from you—
after all, we are publishing books for you!
To request our latest book catalog,
or to be added to our mailing list,
please contact:

CONARI PRESS
2550 Ninth Street, Suite 101
Berkeley, California 94710-2551
800-685-9595 • 510-649-7175
fax: 510-649-7190
conari@conari.com
www.conari.com